FORGIVING
IS
THE ONLY REAL
SOLUTION TO
VIOLENCE

Nancy H. Glende

Noelani Publishing Company, Inc.
P.O. Box 24029
Cleveland, Ohio
44124-0029

Kind acknowledgment is given for the following permission:
Pamela Levin for Think Structure as shown in *Becoming The Way We
Are* used on p. 141, "Think Structure"

Author Photo Copyright © 1993 by Eric A. Glende, Jr.

Cover Design by Nancy Burgard
Cover Illustration Copyright © 1994 by Nancy Burgard
Stained glass crafted by William Greenberg
Cover Color Photography by Thomas R. Malone

Printed in the United States of America

Library of Congress
Catalog Card Number: 94-66011

Published by
Noelani Publishing Company, Inc.
P.O. Box 24029
Cleveland, OH
44124-0029

Publisher's Cataloging in Publication
(Prepared by Quality Books, Inc.)

Glende, Nancy H.
    Forgiving is the only real solution to violence / Nancy H.
Glende
    p. cm.
    ISBN 0-9636216-6-1
    1. Forgiveness. 2. Violence--Moral and ethical aspects.   I.
Title
BF637.F67G54 1994   158'.2
                                              QB194-561

NOTE

This book is meant to inspire, include, and unite people. Principles included here are universal. The author used *The Holy Bible (New International Version,* ©1984 by The Zondervan Corporation, Grand Rapids, Michigan) as a reference believing it to be the most familiar resource to the most people. The ideas are her personal interpretation and understanding from having learned how to make the transition from darkness to light, and having led many others in their waking process.

We believe that *Forgiving Is the Only Real Solution to Violence* is compatible with, augments, and enhances current understanding of major religious teachings. It is our hope that you are one who is ready to be empowered in your forgiving process. It is our intent that you receive specific how-to information. Any helpless despair you feel about growing violence in our world will be dispelled by putting these simple skills into practice.

Throughout this book, in places where the information helps to clarify points, the author demonstrates the message of the book by following through her own forgiving process with feelings aroused in the process of writing it. Dialogs were written directly into this book and are genuine.

The author has used all methods, processes, and exercises in this book for her own growth as well as for facilitating the growth of individuals and groups. She has given information simply and clearly to assure proper application. Used as intended, these tools and guidelines are completely safe. Neither the author nor the publishing company will assume responsibility for any problems that arise due to lack of understanding of the healing process.

Noelani Publishing Company, Inc.

Another Book by Nancy H. Glende -

Sharing the Course: A Guide to Group Study and Individual Application of Spiritual Principles,
Noelani Publishing Co., 1993, Cleveland, Ohio
ISBN 0-9636216-9-6

Accompanying Music on Audio Cassettes
by Michael D. Root, Music of Miracles -

Musical Companion to Sharing the Course
Piano with male and female solo voices
Includes songs for easy sing-along and meditation

No More Blame: A Musical Process of Forgiving As a Way Out of Violence
Excerpts from *Musical Companion*
Piano with male and female solo voices
Includes songs for easy sing-along and meditation

"I'm Safe to Be Who I Really Am"
"I Say "No"
"No More Blame"
"Sigh - The Crisis Is Over"
"Rocking Song - A Lullaby"
"Tender and Innocent (Song of the Inner Child)"
"Love and Joy"

Every choice to blame others,
to believe we are guilty when they blame us,
or to blame ourselves,
is an act of violence to our own soul.

DEDICATION

To the One who invites me to See

In Seeing, I choose to Serve

WITH HEARTFELT GRATITUDE

To the multitude of authors who gave freely to me
and guided my awakening

In return, I extend a hand to you

ACKNOWLEDGMENTS

I am grateful to:

The One who taught me that Father's Love is available to me through forgiving.

To God for taking care of me as a child when I was a child and for taking care of me as a grown-up now that I have grown up.

All the people with whom I have had problems. You reflected to me where I was restricted that I might choose to set myself free.

All of you who chose to set yourself free of restrictions when you had problems with me. Your choices enabled us to be together in loving ways.

Artisans Nancy Burgard and William Greenberg of NORTHERN LIGHTS Stained Glass, Inc. for your gifts of glass design and craftsmanship on the cover.

Nancy Burgard for your gifts in the cover layout.

Eric Glende for your gifts in the author photo.

Paula DePasquale, editorial assistant, for engaging so deeply and devotedly with me to learn lessons of forgiving that we might share this message with integrity. Thank you for your insightful analogy of the plant seeking to grow to light.

Beverly King, my sister, who shared the "dad" events I healed in writing this book. Thank you for being willing to remember these events with me, that you might gift all of us with your ability to copy edit.

Bruce Sherman for your willingness to give your gift of attention to detail as a copy editor to help see to the excellence of this book.

Those of you who gave your abilities as readers:
Mary Beth Biederman, Joseph Gillick, Eric Glende, William Greenberg, Bob Javorsky, Martha Knopf, and Michael Root.

Eric Glende, my best friend. I thank you for being forgiving that you might be kind and gentle to me. My faith in a gentle world begins with you. I also thank you for being in my life with skills that are complementary to mine that we might share this message of forgiving with the world.

Fellow students who expand the circle of gentleness by courageously living this message in the world.

BookCrafters of Chelsea, Michigan, for your excellence in producing this book.

PREFACE

In 1993 I wrote and published *Sharing the Course* and mailed a copy to the producer of a morning television show in Cleveland, Ohio. In December of that year, she called and asked me how a mother forgives when a daughter has been killed. I was surprised both by her asking this question of me, and by the question itself. My mind went into struggle. In writing *Forgiving Is the Only Real Solution to Violence*, I not only saw how to forgive, but also why forgiving is the only wise choice no matter how hurtful a violation is to us. After clearly seeing both why and how to forgive, my mind came to rest.

As I review my life, I see that people and institutions have violated me and invited me to respond with blame. In my younger years, I knew no better. I blamed, and I felt guilty from the blame of others. I now see that every choice to blame others and make them wrong, or to feel guilty when they blame me and make me wrong, is an act of violence to my own soul. Both of these deny my soul its rightful nature to grow. No one had named this as violence for me.

Forgiving Is the Only Real Solution to Violence is about this violence we do to ourselves. Blaming both others and ourselves violates our own soul. It is our own distraction to blame that we heal to fulfill our deepest urge, to forgive that our soul might grow.

We have lived for centuries with a definition of forgiveness that hasn't brought peace to ourselves or to earth. This book reverses the usual focus from what others have done to us, to what we must do for ourselves. To save our souls, there is only one choice. No matter what violations affect our life, our choice to nurture ourselves, rather than blame others, is the only real solution to violence.

Nancy Glende

iii

THIS BOOK IS FOR YOU IF YOU

♦ feel helpless or frightened by violence

♦ want to see an end to violence

♦ feel empty, deprived, or unhappy

♦ are tired of addictions

♦ are living in guilt and ready to find a better way

♦ are tired of blaming and want relief from being blamed

♦ want to know more about growing spiritually

♦ are curious about your soul

♦ value meaningful living

♦ appreciate truthful information

♦ welcome specific how-to steps

♦ cherish the strength of gentleness

♦ like doing things for yourself rather than trying to get others to change

♦ want to learn how to forgive from an inspiring model

♦ want to do something about violence in the world - want to live in a gentle world

TABLE OF CONTENTS

PART III REVERSING INTENT

PART IV   PRACTICING FORGIVENESS

INTRODUCTION

BEING ON PURPOSE

And we know that in all things
God works for the good of those who love him,
who have been called according to his purpose.
Romans 8:28

Have you ever watched a house plant grow by a window? Someone, perhaps you, provides the plant with soil and water, and places it near a window within reach of the sunlight that it needs to grow. Nature provides that sunlight and it seems that there is nothing more to growing a plant. If you look closely, there is more.

The plant reaches, bends, and twists toward the sunlight, as if to grab every speck of light it can get. If the plant didn't do this, it would not grow well. If the plant turned away from light, it would weaken, perhaps even die. The plant, then, plays a role in its own growing. And so it is with us.

We grow ourselves. We grow in qualities such as wisdom, understanding, kindness, gentleness, and happiness with ever increasing capacity to fulfill our heart's desires or else we just get older. Others bring us into the world and provide us with food, shelter, and things we need to know to survive physically. Our heredity, our surroundings, and our experiences influence us. Still, at every given moment, we decide who we are, how we grow, and who we become.

Interestingly, scientific studies have proven that plants that are talked to, cared about, prayed for, and even played gentle music, grow better than plants that are simply tended at the

1

physical level. Love plays a role in growth, in plants and in people.

All plants follow Universal Law which is to grow. They are compelled to grow toward light. One big difference between plants and people is that we have free will. We are called to light at every moment, and we are also free to turn away from it at any time. Though we hurt ourselves by doing this, we are still free to turn away. When we feel unloved and unworthy of love, we are hiding from light. Plants, on the other hand, lacking self-knowledge, do not judge themselves and do not make themselves unworthy of light.

Our soul is our connection with the same life force that inspires plants to grow. It is the nature of our soul to receive light, love, or inspiration from Spirit. We are nourished as we open to receive light and love from this force. At every given moment, we are deciding whether to reach toward light to nurture, enhance, and extend our soul, or to turn away from it and shrink, hide, and diminish our abilities. We decide whether to grow or just to age and die, whether to welcome God, or to banish ourselves from the Garden of Eden.

Eden represents a place where we are blessed with luxury, pleasure, and delight. It is a place where old age, sickness, violence, and death are not known. Eden is a productive state of mind in which we are aware of ourselves as a soul. In this state of mind grows the tree of knowledge of good and evil, our capacity to discern whether we are turning toward light or darkness. Choosing light, we become enlightened. It is a state of our soul.

Like plants, we are rooted in earth. We have a physical existence with a history in time. Despite any adversity from our growing-up years, we are invited to gently turn to light and goodness. Mastering our ability to discern enables us to choose goodness and bless ourselves by living a spiritual life. *Forgiving Is the Only Real Solution to Violence* is written with contrasts between light and darkness, harmlessness and harmfulness, gentleness and violence to help you make choices to grow in harmony with God.

Forgiving is the process of growing spiritually. It is a process to which I am devoted. In my first book, *Sharing the Course,* I shared with readers knowledge and practices accumulated over the years from healing myself and assisting others in counseling and teaching settings.

At a time when it seemed that my life would be only joyful, I lived with a nagging pain in my back. In the writing of *Forgiving Is the Only Real Solution to Violence,* I realized a place where I was still turning to darkness instead of light. In earlier chapters, I describe the different results when we choose darkness or light. Then in later chapters, I use my own situation to demonstrate various practices for forgiving. The written dialogs are my actual spiritual work at the time.

In *Forgiving Is the Only Real Solution to Violence,* it is my intent to thoroughly make one point and only one point. We make the choice to turn away from light or toward it at every moment. The choice to turn away from light and love turns our energy to violence. The choice to turn to light and love turns our energy to gentleness.

When we live only as a body and deny our soul, we turn away from light and seek sustenance from people in order to survive. We blame those others for every discomfort and unhappiness we have while in darkness. Aware of ourselves as a soul, we turn to light and seek sustenance from God in order to live, love, and be happy. We then extend ourselves to others lovingly and have meaningful relationships with them. For all the goodness in our life, we express gratitude to God.

Forgiveness is symbolized by the lily which welcomes light. Forgiving is correcting our direction so we too welcome light in each place that we once turned to darkness. It is our purpose. In the choice to be ON PURPOSE, we live a spiritual life with ever growing capacity to extend goodness to others.

WE ARE ALL CALLED ACCORDING TO HIS PURPOSE.

PART I

Growing Ourselves/
Growing Our Souls

1

CHOOSING TO GROW

Then you will know the truth,
and the truth will set you free.
John 8:32

Is there a God? What is God? Is God really loving? If God is loving, how can he allow horrible acts of violence to continue? Do I have a soul? What is a soul? Why would I want to know any of this anyway? Perhaps you have asked yourself these questions. If you don't have answers, it may be that you haven't asked yourself the right questions. Instead you might ask: Do I want to be happy? Do I want to be healthy? Do I want power to achieve my heart's desires? Is this possible for me? Is there help available to me? The answer to all of these is, yes, of course! These are all your birthright.

When we think of ourselves only as a body, our purpose is to survive, reproduce, grow old, and die. When it is happiness we seek, we must realize that we are more than a body. Happiness is a spiritual quality, not something we touch with our hands. To begin looking at life from a spiritual perspective, we need only believe that there is an unseen, loving force, that we are connected to that force, and that we are worthy of receiving that love. Usually this means undoing much of what we have previously believed about God, maybe about our soul, and certainly about ourselves.

Our body grows old. We call it *aging*. It begins with birth and ends with death. Our body dies. Growing spiritually is the reverse of this. It is our true life work, our

7

purpose. We call it *waking*. It begins with being deadened and ends with being radiantly alive. Our soul wakens. Flowers bloom to their beauty and perfection. We waken to know ours. We must learn what it is from which we waken.

As children and young adults, we are dependent on others for care. We need to get food, warmth, shelter, attention, love, and approval from others that we are not yet able to provide for ourselves. We develop many behavior patterns designed to see to it that we get what we need. We learn ways that work to get attention. We learn to restrict who we are to please others. We also learn to meet the expectations of parents and society even if they don't fit who we are. Our intention is to survive as a body - in other words, at the physical level.

There is an intention with growing both our body and our soul. This intention is the direction to which we exert our energy. These intentions have opposite directions. **Our first intention is willful and forceful with a goal of *surviving childhood* no matter how severely troublesome our circumstances.**

When survival is our goal, we do not concern ourselves with whether our actions are safe or harmful to ourselves or others. Cutting our wrist to get attention meets the goal of getting attention. Only the end result is important when our goal is to get others to take care of us before we develop the ability to do so for ourselves.

There are times during our young years when we get injured, become frightened by things we do not yet understand, or are mistreated by people. Regardless of why we hurt, we call out for comfort. Many times no comfort comes to us. These are terrible times and we have to find a way to deal with them.

As a way of surviving, we are given the ability to deaden feelings. Those scenes where we need love and do not receive it are automatically placed on hold until we reach a level of maturity where we are able to tend them ourselves. We achieve this by freezing a picture of each troublesome scene in our visual memory. Like snapshots placed in an album out of sight, we no longer see or remember the events. Freezing a memory also deadens the feelings we were not able to handle. We hide feelings both from ourselves and others as blocked energy in our body. **The deadening process is known as defending.** This is a natural process that sets up an unnatural state.

Defending reverses our energy so that it resists the flow of life, creating stress, tension, pain, and sickness. We then project these out like a movie projector projects a film. We "give a picture" to others of what our troublesome circumstances are. Lacking the ability to tell others what is going on with us, we allow our feelings to do the talking for us. We do this to call for care from others until we have the ability to figure out what we need, speak up, and act to meet our own needs.

Our call is a willful demand. For example, as a child I might cry, scream, wince, tense, hold my breath, or even throw up. All of these let others know I need something from them. The intensity of my signal tells them how serious the problem is to me. Fear sends a less intense signal than panic or terror.

We must be in a state of stress in order to project stress. We must be in a state of tension in order to project tension. We must be in a state of pain in order to project pain. We must be in a state of sickness in order to project sickness. Stress, tension, pain, and sickness are not our natural states. Because these energy distortions are unnatural, they get attention from others who become fearful, angry, or sad. Uncomfortable with us, these others act to try to solve our problem for us.

Making others uncomfortable to get them to act for us is necessary for us to survive childhood. Continuing to use these means beyond childhood becomes the violence we do to others that calls for violence in return. By the nature of our defenses, we do not realize our own intention and see only their responses as violent.

When we reverse our energy to defend, we separate from the harmony of God. Without realizing it, we deprive ourselves of love because love is the natural flow of life. We live in a state of disharmony, fatigued by our resistance, neither free to give nor to receive love. Though we project violent energies to others, we feel deadened, like life is an act.

Love flows gently in harmony with God. In a state of love, we feel full of life. In our deadened state, we feel empty. We do not realize that we create our own emptiness by defending. We always blame others, including God for both our miseries and our void. We believe we would feel worthy of love "if only" God and others would give it to us. We believe no one cares about us. We focus on how others have failed to make us feel loved.

Using blame, we try harder and harder to get others to give us love. Our actions are violent. We wait for them to change from our projections. Blaming, we continue to feel empty. We have turned away from light to darkness and fail to see our part in feeling unworthy of love.

Our second intention is for *living adulthood* where our goal is to heal and be happy. We are provided a means for returning to light where we once turned to darkness. This reversal, or waking, is known as forgiving. Forgiving is also called releasing, letting go and letting God, turning problems over to the Lord, or handing problems over to God. Regardless what we call the process, forgiving is the undoing of our survival pattern. These patterns do not dissolve by themselves. Forgiving is something we must willingly do.

Forgiving spells the end of violence we do to ourselves and to others. Forgiving is undoing our unnatural state to return to our natural state. Forgiving stops the process of creating stress, tension, pain, and sickness. Forgiving stops the process of projecting out stress, tension, pain, and sickness to others. Forgiving stops the process of blaming others for our miseries.

Healing is a gentle process that wakens our deadened feelings and tends them with love. Many of us know our feelings as our inner child. As a most basic exercise to begin healing, I often ask people to close their eyes and remember a time when they were hurting as a child. I then ask them what they needed. It is that simple to see the needs of our inner child. **All of us want** someone to see our plight, to protect us from that which frighten us, and to comfort us. We heal our heartaches as we give to ourselves and receive from ourselves these much needed responses.

This is our spiritual work. Instead of using force to try to get others to take care of us, we listen to our own inner feelings and figure out what we need, speak up, and act to meet our own needs. This is natural for us as grown-ups. We no longer need to produce stress, tension, pain, and sickness to project to others with force. As we welcome and respond to our inner child, we also welcome love and God into our life.

We have free choice as to how long we use defenses. Nothing ever takes our survival patterns from us. Forgiving is something we must willingly do. God does not punish us with the stress, tension, pain, or sickness we experience while using defenses. We heal all of these by willingly switching our intent to grow spiritually. If we continue to use resistance and restrict our life force despite all calls sent to us to waken, our body will die so our soul can be set free. **We are not meant to die to free our soul. We are meant to let our survival intention die out. Contemplate this important point. God only calls us to waken our soul and be happy!** We forgive to be happy. Our body glows when we are happy.

There is an identity which accompanies both the intention to defend and the intention to forgive. In our resistant and deadened state, we feel like a *wounded child who has been* abandoned or harmed by our parents or others in society. In our expectant and wakened state, we know we are a *Beloved Child who is* embraced and protected by a loving God and other universal forces. Forgiving brings us back to harmony with God where we know ourselves as a soul. God always calls us to waken from our sleep and know who we are in truth. When we forgive, we do just that and are happy once again.

Growing spiritually is our life work, the growing of our own soul. We have been led to believe that forgiving is pardoning those who failed us. In truth, forgiving is switching our own direction from darkness to light, from surviving to

healing, from willful demanding to gentle receiving, and from wounded to Beloved. We quite typically say, "I forgive you," without looking at our part in any pattern. We also typically say, "I didn't intend to hurt you," or, "I didn't mean to do it." Both of these indicate we are functioning under our survival intention which is hurtful, and we are denying our intention even if we are now seeing our hurtfulness.

Forgiving is the process of asking at every instant for release of our survival intention. We make this choice because defenses resist the flow of life and keep us separated from God, which is our goodness. As long as we believe others have to be forgiven, we are stuck in violence. Our focus must turn inward to release the cause of our pain, suffering, and unhappiness. **Forgiving is marked by our saying, "I see, or I acknowledge that I have been trying to get love (or attention) from you in hurtful ways."** This choice to turn inward and correct ourselves is a choice that impacts our life and the lives of others in incredibly powerful ways. It ends our violence.

CHOOSE TO GROW AND SET YOURSELF FREE.

2

RECEIVING OUR GIFT FROM GOD

And a voice came from heaven:
"You are my Son [Child], whom I love;
with you I am well pleased."
Luke 3:22

While we live with a view of being a victim of others, a magnificent process is taking place at the spiritual level outside of our awareness. Each time that defending is the best way we have of taking care of ourselves, God always responds. We don't realize this at the time of course. We only learn this by believing such a thing could be possible and opening to receive this response from God.

God provides the exact complement to our void. It is the part of us that remembers every unfinished scene, knows what we need, and has the ability to fill our void. In other words, whatever we needed from others that they were not able to give us grows in us as our own ability. This complement waits outside of our awareness for our willingness to receive it. **It is known as the Holy Spirit or Higher Self, the loving spirit within us, that which flows with life and encourages our growth. We are given this gift so that we can heal and be fulfilled.**

During the time that we identify as a wounded child, we listen to various voices in our mind that make us wrong, tell us we aren't good enough, discourage our development, and make us feel guilty or bad in other ways. It is in forgiving that we switch to listen to the voice of the Holy Spirit or Higher Self. Forgiving is much like switching stations on the radio from the pounding of hard rock to the gentleness of soft favorites. The new voice speaks to us kindly, lets us know it is pleased with us, encourages and guides our development, and helps us no matter what our problems might be. This voice knows who we are as unique individuals and remembers that we gave up being ourselves to please others. So, we are now encouraged to return to be who we are truly meant to be.

We all have harsh parental voices in our minds. As part of growing, we must realize that we can stop these repetitions and make another choice. **We all have the capability to use our energy to speak kindly and gently to ourselves.** We have grown up in a world that is far more amenable to speaking unkindly than kindly. Therefore, we have stored more unkind messages than kind messages in our mind. **It requires willingness and discipline to reverse this state of imbalance.**

The Holy Spirit is not so mysterious. It is simply the loving part of ourselves, the part God provided to bring us back to a state of contentment. We need not passively wait to hear this voice. As we choose to speak and listen to loving messages, we release resistance and tap into the Holy Spirit voice. Speaking kindly to ourselves primes the pump. The love we create lets God know we are ready and willing to let go of our survival mode and live the gentler way.

I find the term Higher Self to be more practical in realizing how to switch our intention. We tend to believe that we passively wait for the Holy Spirit to speak to us. And, if we haven't heard anything, we interpret that as meaning either that there is no such thing or that we aren't worthy of receiving love. In waiting for something to happen, we fail to send signals that we are ready to listen.

It is our own speaking as a loving parent to our own inner child that tells our child it is time to switch intentions. Our kind words let our inner child know that it has a comforter now. Our inner child responds to us by opening to our gentleness instead of projecting out pain to call for attention from others. In opening, or waking, we receive the gift of the Holy Spirit that grows our soul.

This seems like the easiest thing in the world to do if it is truly loving-kindness we want. It is what we claim we want. At the same time, to speak and receive our own kind voice, we must be willing to stop waiting for those we blame to change their ways. We cannot continue to blame and listen to loving-kindness. The forceful demanding of attention through blame is tied to survival. **We erroneously believe that we will not be able to get needed attention if we stop using force to blame others. We believe we will die as a result. The opposite is true. We begin to live when we stop blaming.**

When we open to the Holy Spirit, we know someone really cares about us. We shed tears of relief as we find that someone truly understands the troubles we've experienced. Remember, this is the part of us that was built into our mind by God to fulfill our need for love and comfort every time we needed it in our past and did not receive it from others. We connect with the Holy Spirit to heal every spiritual wound from our past.

Problems tell us that our life is incomplete. They arise from having restricted options due to defending. Growing spiritually is the process of solving these problems. As long as we blame, we want the problem, not the solution. Remember that no one ever takes our survival ability from us. While we automatically age, accepting our gift of healing is something we voluntarily do because we understand how life works and seek to cooperate with it. We blame until we believe we are good enough to be loved.

It doesn't matter how big or small the problem was at the time that we defended. The problem was something we did not know any other way to handle. To defend is to defend and to undo is to undo. It is the same process. To heal is to undo our survival patterns. We stop blaming others and demanding that they fulfill us. We stop seeing God as absent, cruel, or punitive and accept our gift of the Holy Spirit. In switching our intent from trying to get from others to receiving the Holy Spirit within us, we bring our life to joyful union with God.

15

To heal is to forgive and come to completion. Our joy is not instant. We waken our seeing to acknowledge our part in separating from God. We waken our hearing to receive loving guidance to freedom. We waken our feelings to tend them with awareness. This is a process that involves many scenes and feelings. As we heal, we stop blaming others for their lack of perfection and accept God's perfect answer for us now.

The Holy Spirit is a gift to us to complete ourselves. Most of us use abilities given us by God to try to help others wounded like we have been wounded and fail to heal ourselves first. We seek out people whom we identify as victims. We identify ourselves as helpers and believe we are helping them heal. Without realizing it, we maintain a one-up/one-down relationship with our identified victims and further their identity as victims rather than invite them to heal themselves.

In truth, we are using our abilities to try to get them to love us and we feel victimized in the process. In this kind of giving, we do not heal our own deprivation because we have not yet opened to receive. In forgiving, we connect with the Holy Spirit and open to receive. Only then are we healed and able to invite others to join us in that state.

Growing spiritually is willingly accepting our gift of the Holy Spirit from God to change ourselves. Growing spiritually is an ongoing choice we make to return to union with God. We either remain unseeing and blame others for our lacks, or we see and forgive to be fulfilled. In accepting that God has provided for us, we see the goodness of God and know our own goodness.

Seeing that God has provided both the ability to survive and then to heal brings us to a state of gratitude. Over time, we answer our questions as to whether there is a God, whether God is loving, and whether we have a soul. We waken to know ourselves as Beloved and realize that we, not God, had allowed our pain to continue. All hope for a gentle world lies within this realization.

I have decided to place an epilogue here. After finishing the writing of *Forgiving Is the Only Real Solution to Violence*, I had an opportunity to experience the power of choosing the Holy Spirit over blame. I believe this example will help you understand the message of this book. I also want you to realize that this incident happened after the personal healing experiences illustrated in later chapters.

Two days ago I had an opportunity to experience the power that comes from choosing to accept this higher way. Driving home from running an errand, I was the third car in line stopped at a traffic light. Unexpectedly, a tow truck rammed full speed into the back of my car having made no attempt to stop. My car then bounced into the car in front of me causing damage to that car as well as to the front of my car.

My first awareness was of the traumatic blow to my neck. I was also aware that within the first few seconds I made every decision as to which direction I would intend my energy. My first thought was that the accident was over, and I had no reason to become scared at that point. My next thought was that the most important thing to do for myself was to stay aware to keep my neck relaxed. I took my time to assure my inner child that I would take care of her in this way.

The driver of the car beside me came running over, announced that he was a paramedic, and asked, How is your neck?" This question evoked images of people who identified as victims of such accidents being treated in medical facilities and fighting battles in court. I said to myself, "I am not one to identify as a wounded victim and I am not one to get involved in emotionally draining lawsuits." To him I said, "My neck is okay." I continued to give awareness to both my neck and my inner child who was feeling wounded.

It is very important that we make the distinction between feeling traumatized by events that are imposed on us, and identifying as an unloved, wounded victim who uses blame to try to get others to love us. We can be wounded without taking on the identity of an unloved victim. I felt tender and wounded. I chose to stay loving and caring to my tender self. Any intent either to use blame to try to get the tow truck driver to be caring to me, or to take revenge against him for his lack of care would have been futile. I needed care to my woundedness and I took care of that directly by not going to blame.

Meanwhile, the driver of the car in front of me first sought to blame the driver in front of her for being slow to start after the light turned green, and then turned to blame me for hitting her car. To myself I said, "No, I won't accept blame for this." To her I said, "The truck hit me while I was sitting still and knocked my car into yours." This statement of truth came from my Higher Self, not from a defensive child. There was no blame in my voice and she corrected her story.

After the necessary immediate steps with police, I was faced with dealing with my damaged car. My quality car was especially precious to me. Nearly two years old, it did not yet have its first scratch. I realized that to reject my car now because it had been damaged by the mindless act of another would be like rejecting myself when hurt by the same. I also knew that to start questioning why this happened to me would be to go to self-doubt or guilt, believing that I was somehow deserving of being punished. Realizing that I live in a world where most people are less aware and less caring about life than I am, I decided to only give love to myself, and my car.

In this situation, I continue to be amazed by the effect on me of practicing forgiving in the form of giving loving awareness to myself rather than blaming another. My neck is nearly healed two days after the event. I am excited about being reunited with my car when repairs are completed. I am grateful that I have no need for further contact with the person unaware behind the wheel of his truck. And, above all, I have experienced the healing power of choosing to stay open to love coming through me rather than to use blame to try to get love from someone else. I have no doubt as to my worthiness to be loved, or the presence of a loving force in my life.

**THE VOICE THAT SEEMS TO COME FROM HEAVEN
ASSURES US WE ARE BELOVED.**

3

REBIRTHING OURSELVES

Yet to all who received him,
to those who believed in his name,
he gave the right to become children of God --
children born not of natural descent,
nor of human decision or a husband's will,
but born of God.
John 1:12-13

Our body holds pain until we tell our truth, the truth of our innocence. To be innocent is to identify as a Beloved Child of God. To identify as Beloved is to believe in his (God's) name, or in his way as the way to peace and happiness. The purpose of all learning is to abolish beliefs that stand in the way of this truth.

Being innocent does not mean that we have never done anything bad in our life. Everything we do while defended is harmful in some way. **Innocence is the state of our soul in relationship with God.** When we hold blame, we are identifying as a body in relationship with people. In this defensive state, we are non-receptive to love and light from God. **Being innocent means we have released blame and are once again receptive to love and light. Obviously, as we receive love and light, we no longer live in the darkness of guilt, and know our innocence instead.**

Innocence is like the chicken and the egg. When we are defended, it seems to us that the way to innocence is to assign blame to others to free ourselves of our guilt. Assigning blame puts the chicken first. We never get to innocence that way. We must simply accept our innocence as a soul and stop trying to make others guilty. **We do not get to light by passing our darkness to others. We get to light by accepting light for ourselves.** Accepting light puts the egg first. Let's start there.

To be born of God, or reborn, means we identify as a Beloved soul and accept love and light from God. As long as we imply or say to others, "If it weren't for you," or, "If only you would change," we are not yet reborn. As long as we seek to fix or take revenge against those who haven't loved us, we are not yet reborn. Until reborn, we are not receptive to the love of God.

Rebirth from body identity to spiritual identity is a choice we make continuously. It is a lifelong process, not something we do once. Since our whole world view has been based on our defensive adaptation, our entire way of thinking must be reversed. It is a major shift of perspective like seeing that a glass is half full rather than half empty. Our focus shifts to what *is* there rather than to what *isn't* there. And we look in a different direction, to ourselves rather than to others. Our path to love is provided within us.

Spiritual rebirth joins our inner parent/Higher Self and inner child/Beloved Child. Paradoxically, we go backward to go forward. We reclaim, redeem, or save our energy placed in defenses while we identify as a body in relationship to people. We experience rebirth every time our inner child releases blame against someone else to receive our own love. With it comes a sigh of relief and release of tightness at the center of the chest, our heart center where we both carry our grief and feel divine love. Divine love always brings miracles to us. Miracles result from releasing our resistance to the love of God.

Early life scenes do not come to our awareness until we are ready to heal them. Their coming tells us we are ready. We need to be mindful of the fact that these scenes took place many years ago and we lived through them. At this point we are only healing our emotions left on hold.

I have included in this chapter a birthing, a joining, and a releasing experience. In the birthing experience, you imagine yourself at your birth and receive your inner child as a soul. In the joining experience, you catch your waking child up on what has been going on in your life while it slept. In the releasing experience, you take over the job from the child who defended to survive and set yourself free.

In doing any of the following practices, find a time and place to be alone, quiet, and undisturbed. Of course it is fine to have someone with you who is assisting you or being supportive while you do your spiritual work. If gentle music appeals to you, have some playing in the background. I always have a journal close by to capture insights.

Each of these experiences may be repeated for deeper meaning and feeling. Over the years, I have had a major focus on correcting one area of my life at a time. I find that as I correct each area of my life, I need to release the survival child in that area. For example, I studied: how I related in my family as daughter, sister, wife, and mother; my relationship with the work environment; my relationship with the church; my relationship with money; my patterns of giving and receiving gifts; my whole pattern of selecting, purchasing, preparing, and eating food; my whole pattern of getting sick and seeking medical care; how I felt toward my body, dress, and the use of make-up; and how I viewed myself and others as sexual beings. Within each area, I released patterns that I learned defensively in order to live at a higher level.

BIRTHING YOUR INNER CHILD

Using your power of imagination, have a small pillow close by, sit quietly with yourself, and gently close your eyes. Picture your birth scene. Be aware of what people say about you. (Any words of rejection relate to feelings which you will want to heal in joining with your newborn.) Now take the infant into your arms (take the pillow sitting beside you) and embrace this child warmly. Welcome yourself as a soul. Say things like, "You are a precious soul," "I adore you," "I am here to love the unique person you are," "I love holding you in my arms," "I'm delighted that you are a girl - or - I'm delighted that you are a boy," "I see that you have/are (any physical deformity, sexual preference, or minority which has received prejudice) and want you to know you are complete as a soul," "Come with me, this is our time to be together," "I love you, I really love you," and, "I welcome you into my life." It is natural for tears to flow in this joining.

When we have rejected ourselves for many years, it may seem unnatural to speak lovingly to ourselves. It takes spiritual discipline to build these positive messages into our thinking structure. Doing so "recharges" us and allows the energy of God to flow through us once again. We were never meant to be dead batteries!

JOINING WITH YOUR INNER CHILD

Using your power of imagination, picture your inner child at some young age. Age five is a typical choice. As your inner child wakens from its sleep, you greet it. Listen to this conversation between my Higher Self and Little Nancy. Say to your inner child the things I say here to Little Nancy. Listen and respond according to how your child responds. You might want to use two chairs for the different voices, or hold a pillow to represent your inner child.

HS- Hi! I'm the grown-up you. You are the little me.

LN- Hi! (said hesitatingly)

HS- I'm the thinking part of you (I point to my head) and you are the feeling part of me (I point to my solar plexus). The two of us are one. And, since I am part of you, I will be with you everywhere you go as long as you live.

LN- (still hesitating, not sure what this is all about)

HS- I take over where your mom left off in her ability to love you. I take over where your dad left off in his ability to love you. I am the one you have longed for to make you feel loved. That is my job.

LN- Well, that sounds good. I need someone to love me.

HS- I do love you, Nancy. I really love you.

LN- I really don't know what that means (said skeptically). I don't know what it would be like to be loved.

HS- Yes, I understand that you don't.

LN- Will you leave if I don't understand?

HS- Of course not. I want to be with you and talk to you. I want to play with you.

LN- No one talks to me. No one even sees me.

HS- I see you, Nancy. That is why I am talking to you. I hear you, too. That is why I am responding to you.

LN- Oh. [Note the shift of energy here when Little Nancy realizes she is seen and heard.] Well, how can you play with me? You are a grown-up. Grown-ups don't play with kids. They work.

HS- [Note that Little Nancy needs some new information for the grown-ups she knew when she defended worked hard and did not play with her.] It is true that grown-ups work and they also play. When the two of us are together, we will feel light-hearted. That feels playful. Do you think you would like that?

LN- Sounds better than all the bad feelings I've had.

HS- I'm here to take care of your feelings so you can feel good and play, Nancy.

LN- I've never had anyone to take care of my feelings. I don't even know what you mean.

HS- I'm glad you tell me when you don't understand something so I can tell you. What I mean is that when you are mad or frustrated it means something isn't right for you. You need something. It is my job to figure out what you need and take care of the situation for you.

LN- Will you be angry with me when I don't know how to do something?

HS- No, I am here to help you do whatever you have to do.

LN- Will you hit me?

HS- Never, Nancy. I only help you.

LN- Will you criticize me?

HS- Never, Nancy. I only help you.

LN- Why don't you get mad?

HS- I am the loving Spirit within you. I come from God and I am not limited by fear. Parents are people just like you. They have defended just like you. And they blame. I don't blame you for anything.

LN- You won't tell me I'm bad and that things are my fault?

HS- No, Nancy. If there is a problem, I am here to provide a solution to the problem, not to hurt you. I see what you need.

LN- I think this sounds too good to be true.

HS- I know it is very different than what you are used to in your life.

LN- Sure is!

HS- Nancy, when you are scared, it is my job to give you new information.

LN- Like what?

HS- Like I just told you how I will help you with your feelings. I told you that I only help. I do not blame. I see your goodness. I see how people defend and blame. I see that all of your life you have been accused of things that you didn't do. All of those people were blaming you because they were not connected with their Higher Self that could love them. They were trying to get you to love them.

LN- It sure didn't feel like they wanted love. I thought they just wanted to hurt me.

HS- Yes, I know. Blame feels that way. You have blamed people, too.

LN- Yes. I blamed them for hurting me. Did I hurt them, too?

HS- Yes. It doesn't make much sense to blame if it is love you want does it?

LN- No. There doesn't seem to be much love in the world though.

HS- It is true that there could be a whole lot more if people would be willing to stop blaming and talk with their own Higher Self.

LN- Well, you seem nice.

HS- I am nice, Nancy.

LN- How do I know you won't leave me.

HS- I am part of you. I won't leave you. If you forget that I am here and go back to blaming others you won't know I'm here. You will think I left and even blame me. Actually, you are the one who has a choice. You can blame others to try to get them to love you or be here with me.

LN- I like the way you talk to me and answer my questions.

HS- Nancy, I am going to keep talking to you. My voice will always sound like a friend to you.

LN- I haven't ever had a real friend.

HS- I believe that. I also believe that you know a friendly voice when you hear one and know the difference between listening to a hurtful voice and listening to my voice.

LN- I think so.

HS- Are you willing to stay with me and know you are loved?

LN- What if I get scared and leave you?

HS- I will always be calling you back to me. When you come I will greet you with open arms. I will never punish you.

LN- I feel sad that I have lived so long without you.

HS- Of course. I am also here to comfort you when you are sad. All your sadness from the past will leave as I embrace you.

(Little Nancy willingly goes to the embrace of her Higher Self and sighs a sigh of relief.)

RELEASING YOUR SURVIVAL CHILD

Using your power of imagination, picture the child aspect of yourself that found a way to survive. This is the one who has carried out every addiction including acting good to win approval; acting strong to win love; being sick or helpless to get care; being criminal to seek revenge or try to get even; and abusing your body, substances, or others in any way.

Thank this ingenious child for doing all it had to do to survive all you had to survive. Praise your desire to survive.

25

Our ability to survive was provided us by God to use until we become mature enough to make a direct connection with love. If we try to get rid of this part of us, it will get stronger. We release it by switching our intention, not by fighting against it. This means we do not fight against addictions, including sicknesses. We accept the higher way.

Tell your survival child, "You made it!" You may experience a sigh at this time. Now have a conversation with your survival child. Include the following information in your own words and listen for responses. "I realize what a struggle your life has been while you tried to survive on your own. I know what a weight it has been on your shoulders. I know how you have despaired. I'm here with you now and you are no longer alone. I'm the grown-up part of you. I'm going to take over this job now, for it is time for you to live and enjoy life, not just survive. I'll take you under my wing, and you may watch to see how well I take care of you. I realize our jobs are both the same. Your job was to keep us alive as best as you could as a child in the first phase of life. My job is to keep us alive as best as I can as a grown-up in this second phase of life. For every skill you had, I have a higher level skill."

When we waken from our defensive stance to awareness of our soul, it is like waking from sleep. The inner child that wakens does not know who we are as a grown-up and what we have experienced during the time that it was asleep. We must pass on this information from our thinking nature to our feeling nature. Our conversation would be just as if a small child walked in the door and we tell it about our life, our family, our work, our interests, etc. This gains the trust of our inner child and integrates this aspect with our Higher Self. The separation that resulted by defending is healed in this integrating process.

You survived and now it is time to live. Living requires nurturing and forgiving. In following chapters, I give you specific exercises for nurturing yourself and practicing forgiveness.

**YOU ARE A SOUL.
YOU ARE BORN OF GOD.**

4

OUR YEARLY INVITATION
TO FORGIVE

I am the light of the world.
Whoever follows me will never walk in darkness,
but will have the light of life.
John 8:12

The natural year for our soul's growth begins with winter solstice around December 21. It is the day of longest darkness and shortest light. This is the turning point when light begins to increase daily until the balance is shifted to its opposite at summer solstice around June 21. (This is reversed in the southern hemisphere.)

In this darkness of winter, an aspect of our soul which has remained in darkness is sparked by the star of life within us and begins to quicken. This remarkable annual occurrence is celebrated in the Christian faith as the birth of baby Jesus. It is accompanied by displays of Christmas lights. Meanwhile, Jews celebrate Hanukkah, the festival of lights, in which the lighting of the menorah symbolizes the assimilation of increasingly brighter physical and spiritual light. Both of these celebrations are associated with a gifting process.

Yearly, at the time of our winter holiday, we are called to birth a quality that is Christ-like or God-like within us. We experience this as an urge to express a latent spiritual quality such as faith, gentleness, kindness, firmness, peacefulness, assertiveness, inclusiveness, insightfulness, truthfulness, tenderness, harmlessness, confidence, or creativity. Like days lengthening with light, our soul grows in light. As this quality grows in us, it gifts our life.

As the Christ, Jesus expressed God-like qualities when he taught. He was a model for us. We are meant to accept God-given gifts of life and express these qualities in ever increasing capacities as we mature spiritually. This means that where we once used resistance to survive, we are called to be nonresistant and accept God's plan for our growth. We are to let go of trying to get love from other humans and be receptive to what is being offered to us by God.

Increasing daylight invites us to accept love where we once denied it. The invitation comes as an urge to express a quality which nourishes us while we express it. The higher quality replaces what we projected while restricted in our dark survival mode. In allowing our soul to grow, we receive more love in the process of giving our God-like quality to others.

The commercial focus of winter holidays leads us to believe that purchased gifts we give and receive make us feel loved. Perhaps there is no time when we feel despair more deeply than during these times when we carry out gift-giving traditions with an external focus. In trying to please others or be pleased by others in gift exchanges, we miss the call from God and fail to accept the invitation that would nourish our soul. We blame others for our disappointment while we miss the deeper significance of the holiday event for our soul.

Those of us ready to find deeper meaning in these holidays look for it. We pay attention to what urges to express through us. We may experience this as something we want to be able to be, do, or have. We change our attitude of "I can't" to "I can" and are supported by universal energies in receiving God's gifts of love. We respond to the call to enlighten our soul and express increasingly radiant light. At first, the birthing quality remains nestled "underground" in our life. We begin to feel it in the way we treat ourselves. We use it close to home. We do not yet feel safe or ready to express it in the big world.

By mid to late February, we may experience a traumatic period when the seed of light planted deep in the earth of our being cracks open. We may feel restless, like we need to do something and we don't know quite what it is. We are beginning to sprout toward the sun to take on even more light.

And then comes Easter, acknowledged in the Christian faith as the time of crucifixion and resurrection of Jesus Christ. And, for Jews, there is Passover which commemorates their deliverance from bondage. In our soul's growth, these holidays mark the time when we trust ourselves enough to express our newly integrated God-like quality in the world. It is the person we were without the new quality that dies out, or experiences crucifixion. As a result, we acknowledge the end of our identity as a wounded child in an additional area of our life. The new person we are now, including the inherently loving quality, becomes radiantly expressive or experiences resurrection. We know ourselves as a Beloved Child and shine in an additional area of our life.

The Easter lily in all its glory symbolizes the act of forgiving, the reaching to light. In its shape and purity, it gladly welcomes light. As we move further into spring, we go through the same process as flowering plants. We find our space to develop and flourish. We secure our connection with sun and water. The sun symbolizes the protection of awareness, the understanding that comes with enlightenment. Like the lily, we are to welcome light. Water symbolizes our feeling nature which we tend with that awareness to grow and expand. Only through this commitment to life-sustaining forces does our spiritual quality thrive.

We move out into the space of others and, just like plants and trees, we learn to live in harmony with them. Learning to deal with "weeds" in our environment that have a tendency to take over and squelch out tender ones is part of our growing. Often this is a testing time for us. A no-nonsense attitude is essential to allow for full expression of our finer quality. We must say, "No!" to our previous lower ways, and also all invitations from others to respond in ways we did before advancing our soul.

Summer is our time to bloom in full glory. By then we feel safe and joyful with our new quality. We experience the results of our willingness to accept God's gift of healing love. We experience the results of our courage to stay committed to a higher way, knowing it is the only way that brings love to us.

29

By autumn, as the leaves fall and a chill fills the air, we are called to turn inward again. By late November, we experience inner struggles which call for us to attend another new quality seeking to birth. This period of Advent heralds the coming of an important event, our own birthing, our own coming out of darkness. We are receiving the next invitation to undo an aspect of our defense system. The annual cycle begins again with an invitation for us to remove blame from others and accept light.

THE NATURAL YEAR INVITES YOU TO GROW YOUR SOUL.

PART II

Forgiving

5

FORGIVING ASKS
FOR JOY

Ask and you will receive,
and your joy will be complete.
John 16:24

We deserve only to be loved and to be helped to grow. When loved and helped to grow, we are happy and joyful. At some level, we know we are meant to be joyful or we wouldn't be unhappy with the way we feel when defended. Those who took care of us when we were young did the best they knew how no matter how poor a job they did, or we believe they did. Their ability to love was not an indication of how lovable or how deserving we were. Any inability on their part was a measure of their growth, not a measure of our worthiness to receive love and help. **Forgiving asks to remove this measure of others as judgment against ourselves. In forgiving, we open to receive love now that we need to grow.**

To the extent that our parents or care givers were still living in their survival mode when they raised us, they were not yet free to love. It is possible that our parents worked very hard at parenting, did their duty as part of their learned way of being, and gave us no love. It is also possible that they completely shirked their duty and gave us no love. When we hear an angry voice inside that says we deserve more love, it is asking for us to respond. In responding to our inner child, we expand limits we once placed on our worthiness based on the limited growth of others. **Forgiving asks to remove limits we placed on our**

worthiness. In forgiving, we give ourselves the love we need to grow.

It is truly marvelous to see how the evolution of souls takes place. Each generation expresses love to the extent of its ability. The "more" that the next generation senses they deserve is a measure of the growth they are to do for their own souls. Each generation is meant to grow in its ability to give love and extend joy. **Forgiving asks to grow in our capacity to love. In forgiving, we extend love through following generations.**

It may seem painful to realize that we were not always loved by those who raised us. This pain is relieved by also realizing that we are never without love whether parents and care givers are capable of loving us or not. Nature provides a way for us to take care of ourselves. We preserve ourselves by freezing loveless scenes in our visual memory. These scenes wait in darkness for our own readiness to tend them. We ask for joy by remembering these loveless scenes and fulfilling our own unmet needs. This saves or redeems us from those dark prisons. **Forgiving asks for release from our self-imposed dark prisons. In forgiving, we fulfill our inner request for love and become light-hearted.**

The generation before us may seem lacking to us. While we defend and blame them, we unknowingly continue to be just as harsh and harmful as they were/are. God responds as a "call waiting" to fill every void. Our discomfort is offset immediately upon understanding this. Accepting the call is asking to receive God's response of the Holy Spirit. We either focus on the harmfulness of others or receive the gentleness we still need. **Forgiving asks to wake up and receive God's gentle response. In forgiving, the harshness of our discontent is replaced with gentleness.**

While defended, we deny ourselves love because our energy is reversed to resist life, God, and love. We do the same thing to ourselves which we blame others for doing to us. Sometimes we stop blaming others and then blame ourselves. This doesn't bring joy either, for we have not reversed our intent to blame. When we beat on ourselves for having carried out addictions, we are still refusing to receive love. **Forgiving asks for love by**

switching our intent from resisting to receiving that which fulfills us. In forgiving, we receive love and become joyful.

When defended, we feel self-doubt or guilt. Typically we say, "I deserve _____," which subtly blames others for not giving us what we say we deserve. Such blame indicates that we are still defended and have scenes waiting to receive love. I am sure you have felt a nagging sense of self-doubt. This indicates you are listening to voices in your mind that convince you of your unworthiness. Perhaps you even find yourself arguing with these voices. Certainly you never feel happy while listening to them! **Forgiving asks to know our worth by choosing to speak from and listen to a voice that tells us of our worthiness. In forgiving, we open to receive what we say we deserve.**

Being defended is living in darkness. Our defended feelings wait in darkness for our own attention. Guilt that we experience while defended is not from being bad. It is the discomfort that lets us know we are defended or living in darkness. We do not ask for forgiveness for our guilt, we forgive to ask for happiness. This nagging guilt which we hate to feel is a gift to us to let us know our child waits. The appropriate response to guilt is to "shed light" on the situation of our inner child. *Shedding light also means extending love. Love is known as light. Love includes the quality of awareness which is enlightenment.* We believe we will feel happy when others love us. In truth, when we give awareness to our inner child we know the joy of our innocence. **Forgiving asks to know our innocence by giving ourselves the needed love. In forgiving, we embrace and cherish our inner child.**

Another feeling that tells us we are defended is anger. Anger is the energy of blame. Anger comes from holding pictures in our mind of times in our past when we needed comfort and did not receive it. We justify anger by defining our problems as being the fault of others. Anger arms us with weapons which we shoot at the ones we blame to hurt them emotionally. Weapons include criticism, cold silence, spite, hostility, resentment, nastiness, envy, and hate. Though we may think we are powerful when angry, we really feel quite helpless while either trying to make others change or waiting for them to change. It is simply not possi-

35

ble to be armed against others and be comforting to ourselves at the same time. In making my choice to give myself care rather than war with others, I often make a gesture of laying down my sword. I do this when I find myself warring with someone in my mind. The gesture marks the point of forgiving which frees me to meet my own needs rather than blame them for not meeting my needs. **Forgiving asks for comfort by laying down swords. In forgiving, we meet our needs and no longer need weapons to use against others.**

We may believe that removing blame from others means we take blame on ourselves. When we properly define our problems, this is not true. Seeing our problems as early life feelings waiting for our attention does not make us bad for having them. Proper defining brings the solution within our own power. That solution is to tend our feelings. Blame is power that antagonizes others. Power used to meet our own needs is gentle strength, the power of God or of goodness. Properly defining our problems gives us the power we need to solve them. **Forgiving asks for release of the anger and helplessness we feel related to trying to change others. In forgiving, we empower ourselves to solve our problems.**

While defended, we feel deprived and in actuality we deprive ourselves. We experience this as having a grievance against someone else. In truth, we live in a state of grief from self-imposed sacrifice. Perhaps we feel like a martyr tending needs of others and waiting for them to see our goodness and respond in kind. Perhaps we believe we are paying the price for what others have done to us. Perhaps we wear a chip on our shoulder and walk around serious and sullen. Perhaps we fear others and are withdrawn in gloom. God does not demand sacrifice of us. Others cannot make us sacrifice without our cooperation. **Forgiving asks for an end to our self-imposed sacrifice, realizing there is no price we need to pay for love. In forgiving, we allow ourselves to fulfill our desires.**

In growing spiritually, we become our own comforter. This means we turn our focus to our inner child instead of focusing on how bad others are. As we feel a comforter present for us, we hold new images in our mind. *It is not selfish to give ourselves*

loving attention, because as we receive this love, we stop project-
ing violently to others that they are bad. **Forgiving asks to expe-**
rience the joy of our goodness. In forgiving, we extend our
joy and goodness to others.

While defended, we use our imagination to picture worst
possible outcomes should we open again to love. We perceive
situations in which we are rejected, abandoned, harmed, and die
as a result. Next time you realize that you are scaring yourself
nearly to death imagining these horrible things happening to
you, praise your creativity and decide to use your imagination to
picture the opposite. Our imagination is meant to be used to
build faith. We achieve this by imagining connection with a
higher being. Some of us do this by connecting our inner child
and inner parent, and some do this by connecting with a holy
figure (God, Jesus Christ, Mary, Guardian Angel, etc.). Our goal
is to imagine best possible outcomes from living with love. **For-**
giving asks for best possible outcomes by imagining them. In
forgiving, we build faith and trust in life.

While defended, we use behaviors to demand in ways that
are harmful to others. We do things that scare, madden, hurt,
harm, and call for guilt in them. Such things as anger, criticism,
disgust, cold silence, ignoring, being late, not showing up, not
following through with our word, lying, and blaming others are
all harmful in intent. Behind each is some message that could
be communicated clearly and without intent to harm others.
Forgiving asks for an end to this nonsense. In forgiving, we
see our harmfulness and change our ways to meet our needs.

While defended, we block our vision. This is protective in
that it keeps us from seeing, and therefore, feeling things we are
not yet mature enough to handle. The same thing happens with
our hearing. Unwittingly, we live deprived of information.
Therefore, we do not respond in ways that solve our problems.
Without realizing it, we set up conditions for all kinds of problems with relationships, money, and health. These problems
come up again and again, usually with increasing severity until
we are ready to see our defensive pattern. Only in seeing do we
give a response other than the restrictive one we gave as a child.
Forgiving asks to see how we cause our own problems. In

forgiving, we expand our options by opening to the healing power of love.

While defended, we live in habituated ways. These are our addictions, recognized and not recognized. We most easily see and name substance abuse. There are many more addictions that go unrecognized and unnamed. When we neither recognize nor name them, we also deny their violence. This category includes everything we do to try to get love from others including altering our body, being sick, being a good girl or nice guy, and deceiving to win approval. **Forgiving asks to see our addictions for what they are. In forgiving, we own the ineffectiveness and violence of our addictions and replace them with means that bring us what we truly want.**

Until aware of our violence, we continue to be violent. As we begin to waken and see what we have done while defended, we tend to feel guilty for this. Forgiving is complete when we both acknowledge our harmfulness and experience joy of waking. *Proper release requires acknowledging to ourselves and to those we have harmed that we are aware of our hurtfulness to them.* Awake and free of guilt, we see both the harmfulness of having been defended and our goodness reunited with God. Waking to our union with God is a time of joy. We may or may not be received by others with joy. Their joy comes from their own forgiving. Many times as we wake up, we need to surround ourselves with different people who are free to receive us with joy. **Forgiving asks for complete release of guilt. In forgiving, we both freely acknowledge our harmfulness and express the joy of our goodness.**

Since the process of defending is something that every human being does, there are effects from mass denial. War, mass prejudice, institutionalized poverty, and the corrupting and defiling of natural resources of all kinds can only be carried out in denial. Isn't it fascinating that the word "evil" is the inverse of the word "live?" World peace, cooperative living, fair and prosperous employment, and a healthy planet are the responsibility of each of us as individuals. **Forgiving asks to waken and see the atrocity of energy turned evil. In forgiving, we right our own energy and feel the joy of protecting all that lives.**

ASK AND YOU WILL RECEIVE.

6

FORGIVING DOES NOT
PARDON OTHERS

You, therefore, have no excuse,
you who pass judgment on someone else,
for at whatever point you judge the other,
you are condemning yourself, because you
who pass judgment do the same things.
Romans 2:1

Perhaps the most difficult thing to understand about forgiving is that it is not simply the pardoning of others. You say, "What! What is she saying here!" Yes, I know, this is a very new idea for most of us. At the same time, to learn to forgive we must correct our misperceptions about what forgiving is. To pardon others means we have first judged them as being wrong. It may be true that they have been harmful in their intentions. It is also true that we had to defend to make the judgment against them. In defending and judging, our intentions were harmful too. **Forgiving corrects our part in any pattern. In forgiving, we remove judgment and correct ourselves whether the other changes or not.**

Life itself takes care of our young selves by giving us the ability to defend. We freeze in our minds those scenes that overwhelm us to be processed later when we gain maturity. They are always frozen with blame which is judgment. Every person is going through the same process of life. Each soul is where it is in its waking. In pardoning, we do not see the whole picture and we make our judgments about others true in our mind. Forgiving reverses this. **Forgiving relives a scene seeing it**

differently. In forgiving, we see where others are in their growth, stop judging and blaming, and take care of ourselves with options not available to us when young.

Incidents overwhelm our abilities regularly as young ones. As part of defending, we shift the focus away from ourselves in order to not experience helplessness. In this way, we protect ourselves emotionally. We judge and blame others until we decide from a state of maturity to stop it. Our blame is hurtful to others and we justify this harm to them. To pardon would only focus on what they are doing and deny what we are doing. **Forgiving releases our judgments against others and puts an end to our blame. In forgiving, we bring the focus back to ourselves and give ourselves the care we once felt helpless to secure from others.**

Defenses work by making us unaware. So, when we defend or judge, we do not realize that we turn our energy against ourselves and the life force. We do not realize that we produce stress, tension, pain, and sickness to use as projections to get attention from others. We do not realize that our projections hurt others. To pardon would not correct the problems caused by our reversed energy. **Forgiving makes the shift from trying to get attention from others, to giving the needed care to our inner child. In forgiving, our pain disappears and we stop hurting others with our projections.**

Defenses are like emergency back-up systems. They are designed to never fail us and never leave us stranded. One way they maintain themselves is to distract our focus. For example, if we were painfully ignored when we wanted things as a child, we might have decided that it isn't safe to want what we want. Defensively, we might decide to please others to try to get their approval in hopes that they will someday give us what we want. Now we are seeking approval and are distracted from focusing on what we really want. This is how we end up imprisoning ourselves in addictions which are distractions, and then we cycle to ever greater misery and deprivation. Pardoning others would do nothing to resolve our problems. **Forgiving brings an end to our distractions and addresses our original needs. In forgiv-**

ing, we set ourselves *free from* addictions and *free to be* happy.

Every time we need to defend there is another natural process that takes place. We are provided with a witness who remembers everything we ever needed and didn't receive. This witness is the Holy Spirit. As we waken, this voice has the appropriate words to comfort us and the exact information we need to get on with our life. In truly understanding the marvelous nature of this process, we realize there is nothing to pardon. **Forgiving opens us to this inner voice which is God's answer to our helplessness. In forgiving, we receive the comfort for which we long.**

Added to our intent to blame and judge others is our desire to seek revenge against them. This is the energy of hate and violence. We want them to be brought to justice and punished to pay for their "crimes." In contrast, God's Justice is given to us and brings us to completion. Receiving gifts through the Holy Spirit ends our desire to take revenge. Focus on pardoning others is a distraction from our own hate and violence. **Forgiving gives us from within what we lack from without. In forgiving, we feel complete and have no desire to seek revenge.**

While defended, we believe or make the judgment that others owe us things. We willfully try to take from them, demand of them, or steal from them. This ends when we open to receive from the Holy Spirit because we heal our sense of deprivation. There is a difference between material reality and that of the soul. When we give material objects to others, we no longer have them. In contrast, when we give spiritual qualities such as ideas, trust, hope, peace, gentleness, and kindness, they multiply in us as we offer them to others. We have no need to pardon others for not giving to us when we learn how to multiply what we want to receive. **Forgiving gives us what we want to receive and we give (forgive) more to receive more. In forgiving, we end our sense of deprivation.**

We defend or judge when we feel helpless or powerless. We then aim to render others helpless as a way to feel powerful. From this viewpoint, we see every situation as a win/lose situation in which we want to make sure we win and others lose. I do not just speak here of those who look powerful or one-up to us. When my first child was four years old, I anxiously prepared for my parents to visit from out of state. I wanted everything in the house to be perfect. As I cleaned the house, I confined my son to smaller and smaller quarters until he was confined to his bed for a nap. It was the bed my mother would sleep in. I had bought a new blanket and pillow for the bed. Instead of napping, my son revolted against the imposed confinement by vomiting grape juice all over his bed. I exerted power over him from the one-up position. He exerted power over me from the one-down position. Over the years, I have learned to love myself. I no longer need to go to such extremes to try to be perfect to not feel the helplessness of trying to get love and approval from my parents. I did not need to pardon my son, nor did I need to pardon my parents. I simply needed to look for love in the right place. **Forgiving ends our desire and intent to render others helpless by using power over them. In forgiving, we heal our own helplessness.**

While defended, we tell stories about how others have wounded and damaged us. In the telling, we never include our part in the process. We cannot continue to tell stories about our wounds from a helpless position and accept our healing. We must be willing to tell new stories about our healing and the wonderful results. Just as our body builds scar tissue where wounded, our soul also strengthens. Focus on pardon is focus to the wound. **Forgiving accepts healing growth and shares in new ways with others. In forgiving, we tell new stories.**

While defended and judging others, we do not see all there is to see, or feel all there is to feel in our life circumstances. Therefore, we tend to put up with, excuse, go along with, give consent to, cooperate with, and overlook things, using addicted patterns in response to destructiveness by others. We do not purchase rotten food from the grocery and put it into our physical body. Yet, while defended, we do take in rotten words and projected feelings from others. This is nonsense! Focus on pardon would be aimed at the grocer who sold rotten food rather than our own oblivion in making the purchase. **Forgiving wakens us to see what is there, properly name what is destruc-**

tive, and give an appropriate response to that which is harmful. **In forgiving, we stop going along with nonsense.**

And, I might add, while defended and judging others, we excuse, laugh off, overlook, or may be completely oblivious to our own nonsense. Where I use "others" here you may think of this as various people in your life; as various institutions like the church, medical system, educational system, legal system, financial system; as various places of employment; and as holy figures as God, Jesus Christ, or Mary. Rereading this chapter with a different focus may increase your insight and empower your forgiving. **Forgiving wakens us to see our own nonsense, name it as destructive, and stop it. In forgiving, we stop our own nonsense.**

There are times when we believe raging at those we hate gives them their due, and then we can get on with our life as though nothing has happened. To rage, however, we must first defend. Defenses are weapons of attack. By natural law, when we attack we are attacked. When we judge, we are judged in the process for we must separate from the love of God. Rage is a murderous weapon, a double edged sword, and we are harmed by our choice to use it. We are mistaken to believe that our rage will bring us what we need and then we can pardon the other. **Forgiving enables us to see that rage does not get us anything that we truly want and that choosing to lay down our sword does. In forgiving, we release hate of others and meet our needs to get on with our life.**

There are times when we believe we can get what we want by bargaining or compromising, both of which involve sacrificing. We give up things to try to get things from others. Or, we demand that others give up things to get things from us and set up a situation in which we receive resentment from them. We are responsible for our choices to sacrifice and have no others to pardon. **Forgiving releases our pattern of taking less than is right for us and learning to trust inner guidance for how we are to do things. In forgiving, we move to a stance where everyone wins.**

As we outgrow childhood ways of relating, we release manipulative hooks that we used to get attention. Others may want to keep us behaving within our defensive patterns because they are afraid of our changes. They may continue their side of the pattern and seek to hold us back. When we don't give in, we may experience separation or even alienation from them. It is natural for us to want to be liked and loved by everyone. Manipulation, by ourselves or others, is not love. It is appropriate to accept our own growth rather than think of pardoning others for not growing. **Forgiving stops our demand that others change and accepts our own growth whether others grow or not. In forgiving, we befriend our true selves.**

We have been led to believe that forgiving is pardoning others and that we somehow win their love, friendship, or approval by saying, "I forgive you." We may believe we win approval from God by pardoning others. To say we forgive others as an attempt to win love is trying to "be good" to gain their approval. It is a defensive stance. **Forgiving enables us to accept love of God as a fact of life. In forgiving, we extend love to others and gratitude to God.**

**FORGIVING IS CORRECTING YOURSELF.
FORGIVING IS NOT PARDONING OTHERS.**

7

REFUSING TO FORGIVE IS VIOLENCE (HARMFULNESS)

The light shines in the darkness,
but the darkness has not understood it.
John 1:5

What unites us all is wanting to be safe, loved, and happy. Yet we live in a society that is so far removed from these natural states that we don't even know what is possible for us. Living in opposition to the life force is living unnaturally. Refusing to relinquish our way of surviving to accept the higher way leaves us with no choice but violence. Only when safe and loved do we express ourselves magnificently. Most of us have no measure of what our life could be under those circumstances. More likely, we feel despair about ever finding any place or any one with whom we truly feel safe and loved. We have lived our whole life in the midst of named and unnamed violence. **Forgiving is seeing how unnaturally we have lived while denying our soul. In forgiving, we see from our enlightened state the results of having turned against God.**

The seeds of harmfulness are the pictures we stored in our visual memory. We use these pictures to remind ourselves that no one cares about us. And, as a result, we no longer welcome our own natural expression. Simply believing that we are unwelcome and unsafe to express our life, we restrict our life force and express substitutes (addictions). All substitute expressions are violent. God is not a bad God, nor does he abandon us. We pivot to defenses and lose sight of God. While perpetuating violence against ourselves and others, we call God wrathful. The source of this violence goes unnamed. **Forgiving is correcting the darkness of our self-imposed survival limitations. In forgiving, we accept our natural, gentle, and delightful expression.**

Violence is a spiritual issue. It always begins with perceiving ourselves as unloved and blaming others for this. In blaming, our energy is always opposing the life force. Therefore, in opposing the life force we do not experience the love of God. Instead, we hate others for not loving us. This intent to hate includes God. Hatred begins in the way we perceive things and secondly reflects in our behavior. When hateful, we justify being violent. When we refuse to see God's love for us, we choose to perpetuate violence. **Forgiving is opening our sight to see God's love. In forgiving, we become gentle and harmless.**

At any one time, we intend either to create or to violate. Every intent to blame is a choice to violate. Creating is our natural growth that enables us to continuously give new responses to old situations. We are empowered when we release old habits and give responses that are harmless in current situations. Such responses also invite others to release their defenses and grow. The decision to grow spiritually is the decision to be truly powerful and stop being harmful. **Forgiving is seeing harmless options and having the freedom to take them. In forgiving, we give new responses to old situations.**

We all participate in and live with constant stabs in the gut and back in the form of verbal abuse. This misnamed abuse is the supposed appeal of situation comedies. Projections of hate carried out verbally murder our spirit like guns murder our body. Perhaps we receive more harm from our own self-criticism than from criticism by others. Self-criticism is not harmless, nor does it effectively lead to self-correction. We experience the pain of it in every cell in our body. It is a significant factor in our states of dis-ease. The more violence we see outside of ourselves the more we tend to point a finger saying look at "them." I found that when I stopped criticizing myself, I no longer sensed any need to criticize others and no longer attracted criticism from others. I could see their circumstances without needing to be hurtful to them. We must all begin to see how we harm ourselves as well as others with criticism. There is a better way. **Forgiving is choosing to give information in loving ways both to ourselves and to others. In forgiving, we give information harmlessly and generously include praise.**

There are many signs and symptoms that seek to tell us we are restricting our life force. Some are physical miseries like pain and sickness. Some are emotional miseries like resentment and envy. Resentment tells us that we are hating and murdering our own spirit. We say to ourselves, "I can't be who I want to be." Envy is murderous hate of others. We silently say, "I can't be what you are and I want to kill you for being what you are." Some symptoms are mental miseries like worry, stress, anxiety, and hassling. Medicating these symptoms and ignoring their spiritual message is violence. **Forgiving is healing our miseries. In forgiving, we grow ourselves spiritually.**

Our need to defend may originate as a response to hurtfulness by others. As we grow, we see that the only reason they are hurtful is because they, too, defended in response to hurtfulness from others. Once defended, we attack others to try to get them to stop being hurtful to us. So now we are doing the same thing we want them to stop doing to us. We enter a vicious cycle. The only way out of this trap is to stop our own hurtfulness. **Forgiving is freeing ourselves from the trap of violence. In forgiving, we stop being hurtful and invite others to join us.**

Love does not hurt or cause pain. Violence hurts and causes pain. We do all kinds of things that we misname as loving while we are defended. We try to please, give in, bestow lavish gifts, accept things that are not right for us, give and take unsolicited advice, do more than our share, impose ourselves sexually, fake orgasm, and try to fix others, just to name a few. The truth is that we are trying to get others to love us while actually attacking them with blame. If it hurts, it is violence. **Forgiving is bringing ourselves to truthful expression. In forgiving, we extend love.**

There are only two states possible for us, connected with love and enlightened, or defended and blaming. When we do not feel loved we are defended. Since defenses reverse our thinking, we ALWAYS believe others are at fault for our unhappiness and deny our own responsibility. So, we need to learn that when we feel unloved, we are ALWAYS being hurtful to others in blatant or subtle ways. Whether expressed as resentment, cold silence, or blaring accusations, blaming is violent. **Forgiving is connecting with love and seeing that we have no need to blame anyone for feeling unloved. In forgiving, we feel loved.**

When defended, we experience ourselves as victims of others no matter how violent we are toward them. The numbing effect of defenses keeps us unaware of our own harmfulness. We also numb ourselves to harmfulness of others and make ourselves subject to violence without realizing it. While we identify as victims, we are ALWAYS blaming others and perpetuating harmfulness. Also, since our energy is reversed in blame, we are inviting attack and are not receptive to love. Love is essential for growth. **Forgiving is releasing blame and accepting love to grow. In forgiving, we know peace and happiness.**

Until we willingly choose to heal, we use power over others to deny our feelings of helplessness. Children seek power over others by doing such things as whining, spilling food, knocking things down, running beyond limits, or even having an asthma attack. All of these work to scare or upset others and distract them from what they are doing. Children call for attention this way, not love. For children, these actions meet survival needs. Grown-ups seek power over others by doing such things as criticizing, expressing disgust, discounting in any way, giving advice ("shoulds"), intimidating, threatening, humiliating, getting drunk, and being confused, sickly, or in debt to others. They are also seeking attention, not love. Behind every act in which we seek to use power over others, there is a repressed memory of being helpless or powerless. When we are a grown-up, to refuse to heal these scenes and continue to use power over others is violent. **Forgiving is healing our own feelings of helplessness rather than trying to render others helpless. In forgiving, people want to be with us because they feel safe and comfortable around us.**

While defended, we see every relationship as one-up/one-down. This includes relationships with institutions as well as people. Parents usually see their children as one-down and rarely give the same respect to their children that they offer friends. At the same time, children have a need to see their parents as parents and rarely see them as people with lives of their own. We often feel one-down when the institutions that employ us give evaluations of our work. While we experience them as one-up, they undoubtedly feel one-down in trying to get employees to live up to their goals and expectations. In relations, both with people and with institutions, the one in the one-up position is viewed as having power and the one in the one-down position is viewed as not having power. Neither is true. All defensive stances are masked powerlessness and, in truth, violent. **Forgiving is empowering. In forgiving, we see our oneness as souls all needing love to grow.**

Along with the view of one-up/one-down, we believe that one has to win and one has to lose. The intent in a defensive stance is always to make sure the other loses so we come out victorious. The only victory we achieve is rendering the other helpless and maintaining our false sense of power. Of course, this victory never brings us love which is what we really want. And, revelry from our violence is short-lived because we immediately prepare for its counter-attack. Victory in any win/lose situation is violent to our soul. **Forgiving is the switch to cooperation which supports the needs of everybody. In forgiving, everybody wins.**

We have become a nation with a propensity to enter into litigation. To justify suing, we must first identify as a victim. From this one-down position, we seek to become one-up. When carried out as revenge, law suits are a win/lose battle in which no one wins spiritually. Any system set up to bring justice by switching the one that wins and the one that loses is based on violence. **Forgiving is eliminating our need to be either one-up or one-down. In forgiving, we step aside from both revenge and litigation.**

When we fail to grow and forgive our early life scenes, we cycle downward to ever more dangerous acts. Arming ourselves with guns is no more than the extreme in trying to make sure that others feel the helplessness we don't want to feel. We try to be the stronger one because we believe there is no way to meet our tender needs by cooperating with others. Guns are for killing. **Forgiving is giving caring attention to life and laying aside guns. In forgiving, we cooperate with others to meet tender needs tenderly.**

It is easy to see and name acts of rape or robbery as violent acts. Here, one person wields power over another using physical strength or a material object. The results can be seen and materially measured. However, when others aggravate us by being devious, not keeping their word, or leaving a trail of disorder to disrupt our life, we rarely call these acts violent. There are other omissions which are also violent. They include refusing to pay child support, failing to reveal information about HIV, participating in unprotected sex and using abortions after the fact, and withholding information to misrepresent ourselves in other areas of our life. Passive acts are also violent. **Forgiving is actively fulfilling our needs. In forgiving, all that we do enhances others as well as ourselves.**

Those who sit on pedestals believing they know what is best for others have the unconscious intent of hiding their helplessness. For example, psychiatrists and physicians may deviously keep a focus on patients as the sick ones. The license to prescribe drugs gives them power over others. Whole families may identify one person as a victim (the sick one, the drunk one, the bad one, the weak one, the stupid one, etc.) to mask the helplessness of other members. Whole churches are built around leaders who seek to save helpless sinners. And parents, to not feel their own helplessness, may seek to control the lives of grown children. Unhealed helpers render harm in the name of helping. **Forgiving is healing our own helplessness and therein releasing the need to abuse others. In forgiving, we are safe to be powerful without needing the other to be powerless.**

Going nowhere in life means we refuse to heal the pictures in our mind. Therefore, we stay frozen, neither giving nor receiving love to grow. We needlessly wait for others to become loving first. We needlessly feel stuck. The degree of violence to which we have been subjected reflects the extremes to which those around us have tried to get "love" from us without being tender receivers. Meanwhile, we have subjected all around us to our violence. When we become receivers of love, we grow and extend love as a natural result of our growing. **Forgiving is opening to give and receive love. In forgiving, we get on with our lives.**

Public media currently glorifies investigative reporting which is often no more than justified violence as it incriminates, scandalizes, and assassinates public figures. Bringing up "skeletons" denies that people learn lessons and grow spiritually. Great leaders need to have learned great lessons to get where they are. Meaningful reporting would honor their growth and change.

Justifying violent programming throughout the day because of the potential for great profits is the same pattern as dealing in illegal drugs because of the large amount of money it brings. Both are claiming no better way to get money. Neither demonstrates care about the consequences of furthering violence. Both are violent.

News programs project violence to mask their own feelings of helplessness to financially support themselves with "good news." Instead of using creativity, or even the good news offered to them by people like myself, they claim the public does not support "good news" and blame the public they serve.

Public media is only one institution that involves all of us. Difficult as it may be, we as individuals make up all the institutions on earth and must take responsibility for participating in their violence. It takes courage and devotion to find ways to live in a world of institutional structures and remain harmless. I know. I have devoted myself to this process for years and it doesn't become easier. **Forgiving is opening to feel our natural revulsion toward violence. In forgiving, we choose to focus on that which is courageous, lovely, and inspires greatness.**

**FORGIVING IS CHOOSING HARMLESSNESS.
ALL ELSE IS VIOLENCE.**

53

8

CHOOSING TO FORGIVE BRINGS GENTLENESS (HARMLESSNESS)

Love does no harm to its neighbor.
Therefore love is the fulfillment of the law.
Romans 13:10

Gentleness requires that we neither abuse nor tolerate abuse. When we see and properly name abuse, we are free to rise above it. Still, when we have lived with abusive ways as "normal" and we begin to change, our new responses may not feel "normal." Making the switch often requires going against everything we have learned is right. Abusive ways seem strong and protective to us. We may believe we will be weak and endangered if we give them up. We may believe we will stand alone in our choices or be overwhelmed by harmfulness from others. Truth is, gentleness aligns with all the power of the universe and is the only real strength we ever know. When we are no longer stuck in habitual responses, we are free to move out of harm's way. Freedom to not participate in harm's way is real strength.

Some years ago after doing much forgiving, I still became fiercely driving in nature when fearful. I decided to bring gentleness into my life by imagining myself as gentle, by thinking about gentleness, and by using the word "gentle" in my speech. I had bought a hammer dulcimer and named it "Gently." Each time I prepared to play it, I announced, "I am going to play "Gently." Within a couple months people were saying to me, "You are so gentle." I have remained so over the years. **Forgiving is the strength which sets us free from abuse. In forgiving, we know the strength of gentleness.**

Gentleness requires that we acknowledge the fearful inner child aspect of ourselves. It is this aspect that holds a stance of "I can't" when not connected with our grown-up awareness. This may be cloaked as, "I'd like to be able to ____." In either case, our inner child sees no safe way by itself to meet its needs. Interestingly, when we connect our thinking nature with our inner child, we also connect with God. The law for growth of our soul is that we must see a being greater than we are as capable of loving us, and that we view ourselves as worthy of receiving this love. When we take the hand of our inner child, we fulfill this law and walk courageously together through any fear. **Forgiving is fulfilling the law of love. In forgiving, we are never alone.**

Gentleness requires that we recognize blame and set ourselves free from it. The most common indicators of blame are the spoken or unspoken, "If it weren't for you," and, "If only." While it is true that others harm us, it is also true that blaming harms us as well as others. *We cannot change what others have done to us. We can change our response of helplessness and blame to what they have done to us.* It is our stance of blame which renders us helpless and keeps us stuck. And, as long as we blame, we continue to invite more harm to ourselves. **Forgiving is releasing blame and setting ourselves free. In forgiving, we become gentle.**

Gentleness requires that we be free to give and receive harmless responses. Free does not mean free to be harmful, nor does it mean that we accept harmfulness from others. Free means aligned with God or love rather than with the hurtful energy of defenses. Free means free to see what is truly there so we give responses other than habituated harmful responses. *Free means free to respond in ways that meet our needs rather than against others whom we see as not meeting our needs.* Free means free to give appropriate firm responses to harmfulness. **Forgiving is what sets us free to give and receive gentle responses. In forgiving, we never choose harm's way.**

Gentleness requires seeing and accepting that what we truly want is to be safe, loved, and happy. We must admit to ourselves that we are angry about not having these and that we get none of them by blaming others. We need to be willing to let go of all substitutes, which are our addictions, and redirect our energy so that our needs are fulfilled. We must find the way to gently meet our needs without demanding that others change. We are gentle when we give safe, loving and happy responses to life. **Forgiving is how we become safe, loved, and happy. In forgiving, we do no harm.**

Gentleness requires that we express ourselves naturally. As we heal the pictures we hold in our mind, we see a loving being to welcome our expression. We also see a comforter should we happen to be hurt. We now feel free to BE. Genuineness is a characteristic of those aligned with God expressing love. Natural expression inspires, empowers, and encourages other natural expression. **Forgiving is what connects us with God. In forgiving, we inspire others with our genuine expression.**

Gentleness requires that we know that we deserve only to be helped. When others are not helpful, it is simply a measure of their spiritual growth. When we remember that we deserve only to be helped, we stay intent on helping ourselves. We do not allow ourselves to be distracted into trying to change or punish those who are not helpful because this is not helpful to ourselves. The Holy Spirit is our own Higher Self which knows the specific help we need. Sometimes we know this voice as intuition. Too many times we hear it and do not follow the guidance. Instead, we do things our habitual way. Then, when things do not work out well, we realize that we did receive inner messages giving us a different direction. The Holy Spirit both offers the loving-kindness we need and leads us to truly helpful people or brings them to us. We only realize this when we are free of blame. **Forgiving is welcoming help from the Holy Spirit. In forgiving, we receive the help we deserve.**

Gentleness requires that we shift our intent from seeking revenge against others to being gentle with ourselves. At any one time, we are focusing on undoing our restrictions to fulfill our heart's desires, or we are focusing on hurting those whom we see as standing in the way of our fulfilling them. *Put simply, we heal ourselves or hurt others. To heal ourselves, we must see the hurtful behavior of others without responding with hurtfulness.* **For-**

giving is seeing violence as nonsense and not participating in it. In forgiving, we heal and fulfill our heart's desires.

Gentleness requires that we accept happiness into our life. Happiness is not something we get or something which is given to us by others. Happiness is the delight that comes from correcting our inner separation. To achieve this, we release our childhood ways of calling for attention from care givers and respond to the call of God to waken. When I was young, I used a "serious" look to project resentment and hate. In my healing process, I spent months saying to myself, "Soft eyes, happy face," to undo the tension and seriousness I had built into my face. Happiness comes from helping our inner child give new responses to life situations. Sometimes we have to put on a new face! **Forgiving is doing our inner healing to be happy. In forgiving, we experience delight.**

Gentleness requires proper use of judgment. When we make something good or bad, right or wrong, we are making a judgment. We use this form of judgment to justify blaming. To blame is to defend. So, in declaring ourselves as good and right while declaring others as bad or wrong, we suffer all the results of defending. Discernment, on the other hand, is a higher form of judgment which enables us to see what is there without resisting and therefore ending up stuck in our defensive stance. Discerning is seeing whether things are harmful or harmless. Discerning is seeing whether things are violent or gentle. Discerning is seeing whether things are effective or not effective at making us feel safe, loved, and happy. **Forgiving is seeing without using defenses to try to change others. In forgiving, we discern and choose the higher way for ourselves.**

Gentleness requires that we acknowledge our innocence, our worthiness to receive love. When someone holds us at fault for something, we may also believe that changing ourselves would admit that we are guilty. The tendency is to assign fault to the other ("lay a guilt trip on them"). We believe this assures our innocence. In truth, we mask our own guilt, the belief that we are unworthy to receive love. We end up armed for war rather than innocent. If we refuse to change ourselves, we stay stuck in that war. Healing ourselves does not prove anyone right or wrong. It simply corrects the direction of our energy turned to blame. **Forgiving is choosing peace over war. In forgiving, we are willing to be first to disarm, and to do so whether the other disarms or not.**

Gentleness requires that we accept Justice. We use early life memories in one of two ways and the meaning of justice is reversed in them. Defensively, we use memories to justify revenge against others. In this form of justice, we want them punished because we see them as having harmed us. Our other option is to use memories to see where we still hurt and then open to receive the gentleness we need. In this choice, we accept God's Justice which brings the good to us that we deserve. **Forgiving is returning to what is natural, free, and loving. In forgiving, we receive gentleness through God's Justice.**

Gentleness requires that we never, never, ever criticize ourselves. Criticism attacks our spirit and is the opposite of seeing changes we need to make and offering ourselves the love we need to make them. *Violence begins with this critical voice in our own minds and we must silence it to grow. Criticism is a choice against growth and happiness.* When we accept that whatever we've done is our best so far, we simply see that there is more to learn if we are not yet happy. Welcoming happiness means welcoming growth and seeing ourselves lovingly through whatever corrections we still need to make. **Forgiving is inviting ourselves to happiness by praising ourselves for each courageous step we take in our growth. In forgiving, we know our best is good enough.**

Gentleness requires that we release our restricted responses that cause our problems. These problems include sickness, accidents, and injuries as well as all our emotional miseries. Therefore, we view all problems as challenges to identify our restrictions. With this attitude, we see problems as lessons to learn and people involved in them as reflecting our lessons to us. Only by identifying our restrictions do we set ourselves free. **Forgiving is what brings us our heart's desires and with that, peace and joy. In forgiving, we greet problems and problem people with gratitude anticipating our newly gained freedom.**

59

Gentleness requires that we participate only in arrangements where everyone wins. Until we connect with the Holy Spirit, our life feels like an act. We experience a sense of loss no matter what we do. Life feels real and full when we become aware of our soul. As a soul, we know that we share one purpose with everyone else. Factors we used to separate ourselves do not apply any more. We see no use for one-up or one-down. And, of course, we have no need to use power over anyone. We know that we simply all want to be happy. **Forgiving is living as a soul. In forgiving, we commit ourselves to win in ways that no one loses.**

Gentleness requires that we live by principle. We either live by principle or react to others with habitual responses. When living based on principle, we choose to forgive at any point of tension. This way we make it through harmful situations without getting stuck in them. We achieve this freedom only by choosing how to respond rather than by reacting to others. With conscious choice, we know that no matter how cruel others may be to us we will not respond with revenge. We are truly powerful only when free to take options FOR ourselves and not AGAINST others. It is in taking options FOR ourselves that we fulfill the law of love. *We commit ourselves to be loving to ourselves no matter what!* **Forgiving is what enables us to trust ourselves. In forgiving, we gain trust of life.**

Gentleness requires that we not respond to littleness with littleness. The more we grow, the more we are surrounded by people less mature than we are. If we try to force them to join us, we do so with harmful, defensive intent expressing littleness just like they do. Only in forgiving do we free ourselves to give higher responses. **Forgiving is gently and lovingly inviting others to join us in our growth. In forgiving, we allow every soul to be where it is on its own journey and see to it that we ourselves travel well.**

GROWING SPIRITUALLY IS CHOOSING
TO FOLLOW THE LAW OF LOVE
AS YOUR LIFE WORK, YOUR PURPOSE.

Harmlessness Never Takes A Vacation!

PART III

Reversing Intent

9

A PERSONAL EXAMPLE
OF REVERSING INTENT

Whoever finds his life will lose it,
and whoever loses his life for my sake will find it.
Matthew 10:39

In the above verse, Jesus is teaching us about changing our identity so we know ourselves as Beloved. While defended, we have an entire way of perceiving the world and experiencing ourselves within it as unloved beings. This whole way of seeing ourselves dies out as we accept ourselves as loved in relationship with God. **In forgiving, we let our identity as an abandoned, wounded child die out and waken or redeem our life to know ourselves as a radiant and Beloved Child.**

I was once asked, "What needs to come to completion in you by writing a book?" This is a wonderful question. I never know the answer to this question when I begin writing, because whatever remains unhealed in me is still outside of my awareness. Writing reveals where I am defended and allows me to know more of who I am. In the process, I learn more about being human and share that with you.

I am challenged now to write a chapter that demonstrates the reversing process. My life provides a perfect example to demonstrate this process. **In this reversal, I lose my false identity of wounded child and find my true identity of Beloved Child.**

My dad took advantage of my youthful innocence. He used to drive the car close to a steep river bank and make it look like he was going to drive off the cliff. From my perspective in the back seat, I was convinced that I would soon be plummeting to my death.

Supposedly, to assure that my sister and I could reach a porch roof in case of fire, he had cut a small doorway between two bedroom closets. One night after I had gone to bed, he sneaked through the closet to knock over a bookcase in my bedroom causing a sudden thundering crash in the dark.

My dad was a carpenter. Another common trick was to connect an electrical charge to something like a keg of nails and ask me to hand him one. In my natural desire to be helpful, I received an electrical shock.

One Halloween when I was four, he warned my six year old sister and me not to talk to strangers as we were out trick or treating. Then he dressed as a bum, went behind neighboring houses, and approached the two of us. He called us to him. My sister responded to his lure and that ended our evening of trick or treating. Now I see that a loving option for a dad would be to accompany his daughters to protect them. No one named his violence for me at the time.

[Note: I suggest that you read the story line first and then go back through this chapter to see how I reversed intent.]

While writing Chapter 7 on harmfulness and violence I began to have horror-like feelings in the area of my stomach and sharp pains in a particular area of my back. I experienced them as blows to my gut and stabs in my back. I sensed that I might die at any moment from an attack.

> *Reversal of Intent:*
> *Defended - I project fear to the future that in truth*
> *lies in my past.*
> *Forgiving - I see in the present the fear I stored in*
> *my past.*

In writing, I began to see more, and therefore, began to feel more feelings I had once repressed. I began to identify with Jesus and Ghandi who had reached high levels of understanding about non-violence and then were violently killed by others.

> *Reversal of Intent:*
> *Defended - I anticipate an attack from outside my-*
>   *self.*
> *Forgiving - I see the fear of attack as coming from*
>   *within myself.*

When symptoms appear and we call it "getting sick," our customary response is to take medicine, perhaps go to bed, or maybe go to a doctor to solve the problem. By themselves, none of these is healing. I recognized these symptoms as feelings beginning to stir that I once placed on hold. Knowing that symptoms appear at the point that a healing has begun enabled me to turn inward to look for the scene of trauma.

> *Reversal of Intent:*
> *Defended - I believe I am getting sick and need*
>   *medicine.*
> *Forgiving - I see that healing has begun, feelings*
>   *are moving, and they need to be re-*
>   *ceived with love.*

The symptoms were severe enough that I could not put them off. My stomach was not receptive to food. I felt like I might throw up if I tried to eat. I felt quite vulnerable, like being wounded. That night I told my husband how I was feeling and wanted him to coddle me. He rubbed my hair briefly before we went to sleep thinking he had given the requested attention.

> *Reversal of Intent:*
> *Defended - I seek comfort from another person.*
> *Forgiving - I turn to the Holy Spirit, my own Higher*
>   *Self, that holds the memory of unhealed*
>   *scenes and knows the comfort I need.*

The next day in my inner dialog I was building a case against my husband for being oblivious to what I needed. Trying to be nice while really angry, I once again told him about my feelings and requested that he ask questions to help me identify what

67

was going on with me. He obliged. I felt some relief as I spoke and listened to myself.

> *Reversal of Intent:*
> *Defended - I blame him and call him oblivious.*
> *Forgiving - I waken from my oblivion by asking*
> *where my inner child is needing comfort.*

So, I began the inward search using the symptom that held cues to where I was still in darkness. For some years I have had a localized pain in my back. It is on my right side just below the shoulder-blade. I know it as the back of my heart center. It seems to be the place where I have stored much early life pain. There have been times when my entire upper right quadrant has been nearly immobilized causing restriction in the use of my arm and hand.

> *Reversal of Intent:*
> *Defended - I restrict myself believing this saves me.*
> *I lose physical strength.*
> *Forgiving - I reclaim the spiritual power which I*
> *once gave up and free my body.*

Over the years I have "chipped" away at this problem using every spiritual means I know. I have also had help from others including massage, therapeutic touch, chiropractic treatment, and aspiration with a crystal. Occasionally it still nags and I know I need to look and listen, for my defended inner child calls to me again.

> *Reversal of Intent:*
> *Defended - I perceive the problem as in my body*
> *and despair of the pain going away.*
> *Forgiving - I see that my inner child despaired of*
> *receiving care and reach out to her with*
> *care.*

This morning at breakfast a memory "popped into my head." As a child my worst nightmare was turning off the light at the door to my bedroom and then racing across the room in the dark. Terrified of being stabbed in the back, I would take a breath, brace myself, run as fast as I could, jump into bed and throw the covers over my head. I have never been physically stabbed in the back. However, imagining myself as being stabbed each night coupled with the ritualistic practice of tensing had built the experience into my body.

> *Reversal of Intent:*
> *Defended - I believe the cause of the problem is*
> *outside myself.*
> *Forgiving - I see the need to heal my mind to solve*
> *the problem in my body.*

I have one journal with the title "Jesus Christ" on the front of it. When I am truly ready to heal pain, I remember to use it. Looking upward is praying. In communicating with this higher energy I ask for holy support to my Higher Self. Joining these higher forces gives more weight to my intention to heal than to defend. I also acknowledge the problem as spiritual rather than physical even though I feel it in my body.

> *Reversal of Intent:*
> *Defended - I define the problem as pain in my*
> *body.*
> *Forgiving - I define the problem as being separated*
> *from love in my mind.*

So, after breakfast, I opened this journal and wrote, "Jesus, help me solve this problem once and for all, non-violently."

> *Reversal of Intent:*
> *Defended - I believe I am alone and no one sees*
> *how afraid I am.*
> *Forgiving - I remember that problems originate in*
> *defending and that loving help is avail-*
> *able to me.*

I realize that I have denied full memory of a traumatic event and that this includes secretly blaming someone else for what I have experienced while defended. The pain in my body has been telling me that my joy is incomplete. In bringing secret blame to my awareness, I have an opportunity to release the pain from my body and free my sweet, delightful spirit.

> *Reversal of Intent:*
> *Defended - I secretly blame and this limits my joy*
> *in life.*
> *Forgiving - I remove all blame to set myself free.*

With this principle established and with determination to heal myself, I closed my eyes. I then began to look at the childhood scene of terror. My belief as a child was that a man would attack me in the dark. I have no memory of literally being attacked by a man while in the dark. However, as a child I was regularly subjected to trickery by my dad. At this moment, the fear of being stabbed and his trickery seemed to be one in my mind.

> *Reversal of Intent:*
> *Defended - I am afraid and do not trust my protec-*
> *tor to be protective of me since he hurts*
> *me.*
> *Forgiving - I earn trust of my inner child by seeing*
> *that she hurts and offering her the pro-*
> *tection and comfort that she needs.*

With each act of violence, he laughed at my terror. Meanwhile, my mom also felt helpless when subjected to his trickery. Therefore, she was not helpful to me. I experienced every one of my dad's acts as lethal blows. With each I defended and denied my sweet, delightful spirit. I lived in frozen silence for a long time.

Reversal of Intent:
Defended - I blame my parents for my unhappy,
    deadened spirit.
Forgiving - I see that I chose to defend so I also
    have power to undo my choice.

What was frozen in darkness became my guilt, places where I had not yet been loved. Though I have done much healing around this over the years, writing the chapter on violence stirred another level of emotion waiting for my attention. My seeing and naming the violence brought light into the darkness and triggered my sleeping child to waken.

Reversal of Intent:
Defended - I feel guilt.
Forgiving - I name the behavior from my dad as vio-
    lence toward me. I see that I am inno-
    cent and need love.

I was ready to see my dad's cruel violence without either going into helplessness or seeking revenge. I need only to reverse my response to him to receive love now and free myself from the effects of defending in response to his behavior.

Reversal of Intent:
Defended - I am helpless in the face of his violence.
Forgiving - I empower myself with love to free my-
    self.

Sitting with my eyes closed, I pictured myself as a child running in terror across the dark room. In the scene, I asked my inner child to stop running and turn to see me as I am now as a grown-up. She turned and immediately ran to jump into my arms. I felt tension in my face turn to a smile and sighed with relief. At that moment, I realized that every time I had remembered this scene, I had always seen my young self from the back. I had never thought to ask her to turn around to see me there. Being face to face with my inner child was the key to healing. The child who made the decision to defend turned to see my protective and comforting presence.

71

> *Reversal of Intent:*
> *Defended - I reverse my energy to fear and sepa-*
> *rate from love.*
> *Forgiving - I make a loving connection between the*
> *Holy Spirit and inner child aspects of*
> *myself.*

I talked to my inner child from my state of higher awareness. I told her that she was no longer powerless. And, remembering my presence, she was no longer stuck in this scene anticipating harm and running to bed in the dark. I, as her Higher Self, am her protector and comforter.

> *Reversal of Intent:*
> *Defended - I feel powerless with a void of protection*
> *from parents.*
> *Forgiving - I join within to empower, protect, and*
> *comfort myself.*

In my mind's eye, I brought both my mom and dad into the picture. Keeping with my intent to heal the scene non-violently, I looked at my parents anew. I saw two people, both hurtful to me as a child, and both denying their hurtfulness. Knowing that people who are themselves hurting are hurtful, I pictured guardian angels tending them.

> *Reversal of Intent:*
> *Defended - I believe my parents are mean, hurtful*
> *people.*
> *Forgiving - I see that they need and are worthy of*
> *protection and comfort.*

Continuing with my visualized scene, I told my parents that I would no longer allow my inner child to be subjected to their trickery and oblivion. I removed her from the scene and brought her to my current home and talked with her about her safety here.

> *Reversal of Intent:*
> *Defended - I feel lost in trauma in the past.*
> *Forgiving - I bring feelings to the present and feel at*
> *home.*

With this feeling part of me safe and integrated with me, I was free to look back on this situation without judgment. In defending, I "played a trick" on myself. The emotional pain I once felt and denied showed up in my body. It masked my terror of seeing no one to protect and comfort me. Saying, "My back hurts," over the years rendered me stuck in fear and darkness because I erroneously defined the problem.

> *Reversal of Intent:*
> *Defended - I demand that my parents change to*
> *save me.*
> *Forgiving - I save myself from my terror using God's*
> *gift of the Holy Spirit who remembers*
> *scenes of deprivation and that I de-*
> *fended.*

I then asked myself how I projected the terror I denied just as my parents had projected their stored terror. Two patterns emerged immediately. One was the long-term pattern of freezing my face and showing no delight. The other was the long-term pattern of silence. These patterns both say, "In no way will I recognize your being and extend love to you." Both were death blows to my parents' spirits. Both passively and violently demanded that my parents change to save me. Both reflected my blame of them.

> *Reversal of Intent:*
> *Defended - I believe my parents are bad.*
> *Forgiving- I look without judging and see effects of*
> *defending.*

Willing to see and learn more in this healing, I looked at how I had carried out my defensive patterns with my children. Regardless of how attentively I gave them physical care, my frozen

73

face denied love to them. And, in my self-imposed silence, I carried on my mother's pattern of helplessness when my son was mean to my daughter. I had carried on into the next generation that which had not been healed in the generation before me.

In forgiving now, I step out of these violent scenes with no comforter into arms of love where I am once again free to express my sweet, delightful spirit. I am no longer stuck in a pattern where I automatically react to masked terror of others by tensing my body, being helpless, and maintaining silence. I am free to give a harmless response to others.

I continue to teach others the way to non-violence. I extend love and invite my children to heal. Making myself wrong for my actions when I raised them would only put me back in my defensive mode. **I see violence as the projection of unhealed energy, simply the wounded seeking outside themselves for someone to heal them.** I am committed to extend only love and be a beacon to all future generations inviting them to remain free to love.

**WE ACKNOWLEDGE THAT
WE ARE A BELOVED CHILD OF GOD**

OR

**WE PASS TO OUR CHILDREN
THE PAIN OF OUR CHILDHOOD.**

RULES FOR REVERSING

1. Symptoms appear at the point that a healing has begun.

2. Remove blame which is focus on others and look within for both the cause and solution.

3. Free your mind to heal your body.

4. Look to the past and bring feelings to the present.

5. Connect your inner nurturer (Holy Spirit or Higher Self) and your inner child to tend feelings placed on hold.

6. Simply see each situation anew removing all blame and judgment. Choose a new response in the situation.

7. Take your child home with you.

8. See how you have habituated patterns based on decisions made in the scene.

9. Choose new responses for situations with the same pattern in your life now.

10. Give gratitude to God for this healing process and praise him by expressing your goodness (Godness). (See Chapters 10 and 11 for confessing faith and serving goodness.)

11. Nurture your inner child - tend your tenderness. See the feeling child in every person, the one who only wants to love and be loved. (See Chapter 14 and 15.)

12. While doing spiritual work, if you realize you have a tendency to blame (old identity as wounded child), reinforce your new identity as Beloved by blessing the person or situation and then dismissing either of them from your mind. Have a higher thought ready and choose to think of that instead.

10

CONFESSING OUR FAITH

For in him we live and move and have our being
....we are his offspring.
Acts 17:28

Confessing is acknowledging or admitting the truth of something. The ability to confess truth indicates we have wakened. From our wakened state, we reflect back and see both ways of thinking - truth and its reversal. In truth, we live, move, and have our being within the energy of love. In truth, we are gentle and good.

We do not necessarily speak words to confess. Our new behaviors "speak" the results of forgiving. We may say, "I see, or I acknowledge, that I have been hurtful to you in trying to get love from you." Only after we acknowledge our harmful ways and live our goodness are we free to hear confessions of others. In other words, we listen as they tell us what they did while defended without making them wrong, for we also see their goodness birthing and are free to receive their goodness. Until then, we judge ourselves and invite others to do likewise. Once awake, we welcome and celebrate the growth of others because we celebrate our own growth. **It is our goodness that we confess.**

We acknowledge that we have been giving faith to our survival mode. Our survival mode resists the flow of life and enables us to manipulate others. It does not bring us love. All defenses include secret fears, secret motives, secret means, and denial of their results. What goes unnamed controls us. As we grow spiritually, we name and admit to our fears, motives, and means. We name our ignorance and its results. We admit that

77

living in opposition to the life force leaves us empty and deprived. With each forgiving, we switch our intention from manipulating others to aligning ourselves with the flow of life. **We confess our faith in life.**

We acknowledge that we have been denying our goodness. Along with all of the other reversals we make as we waken, we reverse unconscious denial to conscious denial. Defensively, we deny our goodness without realizing we do it. Consciously, we deny to undo our defensive stance and reclaim our goodness. We choose to say, "I no longer need to believe _____ (judgments I had made against myself or others) as true for me now." It is in admitting that our ways were harmful that we release ourselves from them. We live healed in the present instead of living a painful future based on a painful past. **We confess our goodness at the point that we waken.**

We acknowledge that we have been living a lie. When we turn our energy to resist the flow of life, we are violent to ourselves and others. We live in darkness believing there is no loving God. We live a pretense of seeking love in all kinds of ways set up to assure that we never open to love's presence. Confessing ends the pretense of our first phase of life and puts us in the second phase of life. During this second phase we live enlightened. **We confess our trust in God and know love, peace, and joy.**

We acknowledge that we have been living a false identity. To know ourselves only as a wounded child of human beings belies our identity as a Beloved Child of a loving God. In our false identity, we believe others have set standards that we must meet in order to be loved. We believe that we don't measure up no matter how hard we try. We despair of getting love. In confessing, we admit that love is a gift of life which we have resisted. We acknowledge that we live, move, and have our being within the love of God. **We confess our identity in relationship with God as our true identity.**

We acknowledge that we have been blaming others. While resisting life, and therefore love, we blame others for our pain and our sorrow from sacrificing. Confessing follows our willingness to examine ourselves. Admitting our need to correct our intent enables us to undo our resistance. We do not shift blame, we release the whole pattern of finding fault. Living as Beloved, we align with love and have love to extend to others. Loving is the opposite of finding fault. **We confess our love.**

We acknowledge that we have been thinking contrary to truth. When we reverse our energy to defend, we also reverse all our thinking. Therefore, in undoing our defense system we correct all beliefs used while defending. Every thought must be corrected. When defended, we believe being honest means hurtfully telling others what we see as true about them. Confessing corrects this because we switch focus to honestly reveal ourselves. Honest revealing includes acknowledging our defensive patterns and then the truth, that what we want is to love and be loved. **We confess the truth of our being.**

We acknowledge that living defended is painful and harmful because defenses are double edged swords. We either use weapons to try to get love from other human beings, hurting them and ourselves in the process, or we accept the law of love. *The law of love requires that we view a being greater than ourselves as capable of loving, protecting, guiding, and nurturing us. We must also view ourselves as worthy of receiving this love.* Confessing is acknowledging or admitting the truthfulness of this law. In aligning with this law, we meet our spiritual needs harmlessly. **We confess our faith in the law of love.**

We acknowledge that we have been living imprisoned by our own choice and we choose to set ourselves free. There is no barter involved with this, no demand that anyone else choose first, and no demand that they choose along with us. We exercise courage to grow regardless of what others decide. From this new space, we are able to reflect back on our restrictive survival decisions that caused us problems. With our intention corrected, we are no longer bound by habituated defensive patterns. We are free to take many options at any turning point. **We confess our freedom.**

We acknowledge that we have lived in guilt. In defending, we deny love and believe we are unworthy of receiving it. While believing this, we experience our life as dark. Darkness is guilt due to our reversed thinking. Darkness is not due to bad deeds. It is simply energy reversed to resist light rather than receive light. God does not deny us love any more than sunlight. We pull the shade to put ourselves in darkness and we raise the shade to once again see light. As a radiant soul, we know our innocence. **We do not admit guilt, we confess the truth of our innocence.**

We acknowledge that we use defensive patterns in response to the defensive postures of others and in doing so deny ourselves happiness. It is natural in our young years to respond defensively. At the same time, it is tragic for us to continue to hurt ourselves in our responses to others. We admit our responses in order to correct them and set ourselves free from their results. In doing this, we free ourselves to be happy. **We confess our happiness.**

We acknowledge that we have been limiting what we see based on what we want to feel. When we see no comforter for us, we do not want to feel our feelings. Therefore, we do not accept them. We claim we want to be accepted by others while we are denying ourselves. We say, "I want to be accepted." In saying this, we subtly blame others for not accepting us. To accept is to see what is there. It does not mean we have to like what is there, nor does it mean that what is there is right. To accept is simply to see truth as true and allow ourselves to feel our natural responses to what is truly there. Seeing is essential for us to give a safe, empowered response. Seeing makes us response-able. Only empowered responses resolve problems. **We confess our true feeling response.**

We acknowledge that in defining our problems as the badness of others (including God), we have lived in hell seeking justice through revenge. Admitting our intention to blame brings us to the gate of Heaven. We enter Heaven with tears of relief, sighs of release, and arms open to receive. At Heaven's gate, we define our problems as feelings we need to bring to awareness to heal. And, we also acknowledge that God has provided the Holy Spirit to complement our lack. In properly defining our problems, we reverse our intent. In doing this, we accept

God's Justice and know abundance. This is joyful growth. We give loyalty to the higher way and allow Justice to fulfill our unmet desires. **We confess our abundance through God.**

We acknowledge that we are all equal as souls, as offspring of God. Our oneness manifests as we trust forgiveness as our means for seeing to all we need to be happy. The gifts we extend to others multiply as we give them. We soften to gently welcome the soulful expression of every human being knowing the tapestry of life is incomplete without their full participation. We stop all violence that separates us and offer only gentleness to others. This, and only this, unites us as Children of God. **We confess that our only true desire is to live in peace with others honoring our oneness.**

YOU ARE AN OFFSPRING OF GOD.
CONFESS YOUR TRUE GENTLE NATURE.

11

SERVING OUR HIGHEST GOOD (GOD)

No one can serve two masters.
Either he will hate the one and love the other,
or he will be devoted to one and despise the other.
Matthew 6:24

We serve the disruption or balance of our breath, the interruption or flow of spirit. We breathe in - we take in spirit - we inspire. We breathe out - we express our spirit. The point of our last breath is known as death of the body - we expire. In all defensive patterns, we interrupt our breathing pattern one way or another as we limit ourselves with fear. This serves to interrupt and therefore imbalance the natural flow of spirit through us. We deaden ourselves in the process. Each time we forgive, we release a hold we placed on our breath and allow it to return to balance. A sigh marks the release and indicates that the crisis of resisting the life flow and being separated from God is over. The Holy Spirit *is* sacred breath. Many traditions work directly with balancing the breath as a means of healing. When we balance our breath we are ready to serve God rather than fear. To serve God is to express our highest good in ever expanding ways. Spiritual growth is a sign of true service. **We balance our breath to give true service.**

We serve the restricting or expanding voice within us. The voice in our mind that reminds us to defend always restricts us. One way to recognize our resistance is to listen for "yes but" responses to anything we say we would like to be, do, or have. What follows the "yes but" tells us what our belief is that currently determines our behavior. For example, "(Yes) I'd like to get a new job *but* there aren't many jobs available right now." In this statement, I tell you I am afraid I will not find a job and will end up helpless or dead. To limit my fear, I restrict myself from even looking for a new job. The Holy Spirit voice, on the other hand, invites us to join with it as a friend and grow. Listening to guidance higher than our child's fear, we know that we only need one job of those available. We also know we are loved and meant to receive financial support from doing what we love to do. We choose the voice we serve. We serve fear or love. Serving the Holy Spirit means listening to ever renewing messages that guide and heal us. Serving the Holy Spirit means growing in power to express goodness. **We listen to the Holy Spirit to give true service.**

We serve denial or forgiveness as our purpose. Defenses promote denial of God. They demand that we maintain our view of being incomplete and seek what we lack from others. We further our separation from God and others every time we attack to try to get from others. When our purpose is forgiving, we release the demand on others and turn inward to join our Higher Self and inner child. Our inner joining brings wholeness, also known as holiness. Seeking holiness means giving service to God. We choose the purpose we serve. Living ON PURPOSE ends our separation. **We live ON PURPOSE to give true service.**

We serve illusions or faith. We use our thinking to maintain illusions or to correct them and come to truth. True service is an intent in our mind to correct errors about our separation and wake to our spiritual nature. "In the name of God" means in the nature of God. It is the nature of God for all things to grow. It is our nature as a soul to increasingly take on light. This means that as spiritual beings we unfold to newer and brighter experiences. We waken to see God's plan for us and have faith in the unfolding process of life. Life brings us ever increasing opportunities to serve with ever increasing rewards. *Serving has nothing to do with whether we are volunteering our service or receiving payment.* **We correct illusions to give true service.**

We serve sacrificing or sharing to connect. While sacrificing we perform duties and carry burdens on our shoulders. We live as martyrs with our focus on what others need, hoping that they will give us what we need in return. Secretly we focus on what we believe others owe us for what we do for them. We also resent and hold a secret wish for them to be punished for unfairly demanding of us and not fulfilling us. We know no peace of mind. In sharing, we give what is meaningful and valuable for our soul's growth because we have opened to receive it from our Higher Self. We do what we love to do and are happy doing it. We focus on the quality of what we extend, and we receive direct spiritual rewards for our excellent service. As we give true service, we feed others as we feed ourselves. **We share to give true service.**

We serve slavery or freedom with every thought. Thoughts serve to close or open our hearts. We defend and enslave ourselves, or open and save ourselves. Serving salvation means we willingly allow God to work through us. The results are perfect health, harmony, and freedom. These are God's Will for us. Serving is an attitude integrated into our life-style in which we freely choose to self-examine and surmount limitations to grow. The results make our life experience feel rich. Serving is intended to bring us an income that makes our life feel safe and fair. We are not meant to be slaves to sacrifice. **We save ourselves to give true service.**

We serve addictions or free choice. When we make early life decisions to defend, we also decide how we need to act around others. Our actions, whether active or passive, become addicted patterns to try to change others. Examples include: complaining, walking around with a chip on our shoulder, being a joker, tagging along with others, stealing, regretting, and eating to comfort ourselves, just to name a few. In forgiving, we pray instead of looking for another thing to complain about, joke about, steal, or regret. Sincere prayers are answered and we often misunderstand the process. When we pray, old patterns break down. As things start to fall apart in our life, we tend to believe dreadful things are happening instead of realizing our prayers are being answered. Look deeper. Only defenses or addictions can break down. When gone from our life, they allow space for our good to enter. **We pray to give true service.**

We serve means or ends. In other words, we pay attention to how we reach our goal, or we get what we want without regard for how we get it. When seeking love in defended ways we are indiscriminate as to what we do. We selfishly focus only on what we are out to get without care for harm to ourselves or others. We justify our destructive means to meet our chosen goal. When, instead, our means become our focus, we care about our process and remain unattached to results. We have faith that gentle means will only bring loving results. So, our goal becomes that of expressing our unique gifts of spirit to live their results. Fruits of proper means are beneficial to all. They include: excellence, inspiration, loving-kindness, appreciation, praise, and gratitude. **We focus on means to give true service.**

We serve people or God. In serving people, we seek to win their approval or appreciation as an external reward. Our behavior is aimed at making an impression on them. In truth, God decides the direction for our individual service. In serving God, we honor impressions coming to us as to the direction we are to serve. We welcome urges that lead to opportunities to serve without judging their worth in external rewards. We are contented in knowing that we have a divine nod of approval. We also trust that others are guided likewise and do not judge their service as more or less worthy than ours. Service to God automatically benefits all people. **We serve God to give true service.**

We serve external or internal authority. When we place authority outside ourselves, we find suitable people and act strong for them or try to get them to act strong for us. We take advantage of them, or allow them to take advantage of us. Therefore, in serving external authority, we participate in learned, addicted, and draining relationship patterns which deny our equality as souls. On the other hand, when we follow inner urges and inner knowledge, we are responding to God as authority. When we are willing to have God express through us, our holy qualities strengthen. These include: clarity, calmness, gentleness, kindness, sincerity, genuineness, and a no-nonsense firmness. Empowered with holy qualities, whatever we give is an advantage to others as well as ourselves. In serving God, we extend only holy qualities to all who appear in our life. **We empower ourselves to give true service.**

We serve life or that which struggles against life. We serve wellness or we unwittingly serve sickness. We serve abundance or we unwittingly serve limitation. We serve light or we unwittingly serve darkness. We serve gentleness or we unwittingly serve violence. God's perfection is forever seeking to express through us. We each have our unique gifts to share with the world community. We either serve by sharing our gifts or we add to the forces which disrupt and destroy the world community. **We give our gifts to give true service.**

**EVERY MOMENT IS SACRED. DEVOTE YOURSELF
TO MAKING IT SO IN YOUR SERVICE.**

PART IV

Practicing Forgiveness

12

GROWING OUR SOUL

Blessed are the pure in heart,
for they will see God.
Matthew 5:8

Our soul's growth *is* the process of forgiving. Forgiving reverses our separation from God set up during our period of dependency when we reversed our energy to survive as a body. Forgiving and healing mean the same thing. Both refer to correcting the early life reversal which enables us to once again live as a soul. Our intent in defending was to look to others for solutions to our problems. In healing, we undo this intention to give awareness to our own feelings and solve our own problems. In switching our intention, we see the nature of our being and know our connection with God. This is something no one can do for us. We grow our own soul.

The way to God's love is simply to be willing to stop blaming and do what we need to do to correct ourselves. Our inner child waits for us to see its plight, to protect it from that which frightens it, and to comfort it with new information. We heal our heartaches as we give and receive these much needed responses. As we welcome and respond to our inner child, we also welcome love and God into our life. This is our spiritual work.

Our spiritual journey begins with joining our thinking and feeling natures. These natures are like two poles on a battery. "Juice" begins to flow from our heart when we join our thinking with our feelings. That "juice" is love. We release the need to demand of others by blaming when we give awareness to our own feelings. In blaming, we repel what we most need and want. When we stop blaming, we realign our energy with the flow of life. The pure energy of life flowing through us is God. We become pure in heart.

Purity is free from evil or free from resistance to life. In a state of purity, we feel confident, tender, and receptive. Perhaps many of us resist feeling tender believing we are weak and vulnerable when tender. The opposite is true, for in this natural tender state, we have our thinking and feeling natures connected and feel confident of being loved. We are connected with all the energy of God. In loving ourselves, we also know we are loved by God and are not blaming anyone for any lack of love. Pure and innocent is an empowered state in which we are no longer subject to addicted ways of abusing and being abused while trying to get love.

I have found, both in my own growth and in guiding others, that the gap between pure energy of love offered by God and our defended states is too great to join directly. We first need to develop a kind and gentle voice within us and gain the trust of our inner child. As we open to our own kind and gentle voice, we also open to the love of God.

I find it easiest to begin working with our thinking and feeling natures by calling them our inner parent and inner child. The parent is the thinking nature and the child is the feeling nature. **There are parent and child voices both on the defended side of ourselves and the joined side. This can be confusing. In holding our healing conversations, we need to know *from* which voice and *to* which voice we speak.**

Our whole defensive pattern masks our true child who waits for love to grow. Listening to the various voices helps us reclaim our hidden child. When defended, we listen *from* the part of us that has restricted and limited to survive. We listen *to* the voice in our mind that restricts and limits us. This voice may sound like our mother or father. It may speak as a collective voice for the church or society telling us what we should and shouldn't do to be a good person. We repeat these same messages over and over in our minds and respond in the same habitual ways. These messages are from our past and are not totally relevant to our present. When we listen to these messages, we identify as an angry, wounded child who feels restricted and deprived.

In order to heal, we must speak *from* the loving parent voice and listen *to* that parent voice that speaks lovingly to us. By definition, this is our Higher Self. Whether we imagine what a kind, loving parent would say and say that to ourselves, or hear a loving voice pour forth to us, the fact that it is loving makes it our Higher Self. When we listen to these messages, we identify as a protected, comforted child who feels loved. From this stance, we know ourselves as the innocent child we are in truth and knew ourselves to be before we defended.

In applying the healing methods or practices of forgiveness in this book, you will need to learn to discern the two parent voices. It is rather easy in that one hurts and the other feels good. However, we are so used to feeling hurt that we hardly know what it would feel like to receive a loving response to help us grow. And we are so used to identifying as the wounded child that we don't believe and trust kind words when we hear them. The loving parent voice is something we build in our mind by consciously imagining how a loving parent would respond to us. This is not a message impressed on our subconscious by someone in our past.

We may use some loving person in our past as our model. I've known people to ask themselves, "What would my grandma say?" or, "What would Jesus say?" or, "What would Nancy say if I told her about my hurt?" Asking this helps them imagine a loving response to give to their inner child. **I believe whether we have known a loving person or not, we all know deep within our beings the words we long to hear. We can also speak them. They are the words that heal our separation. Once we reverse our energy and heal our separation, we begin to hear directly from holy voices (Holy Spirit, Christ, God, or any name by which these are known).**

At first we may feel like we are pretending as we hold healing conversations. This is natural. What we are doing is preparing ourselves to receive higher energy. The energy of joining is a higher energy than that of resisting. Through practice we grow in our ability to connect with higher energy.

The most frequent mistake that people make when beginning these dialogs is speaking from their critical voice believing they are nurturing their inner child. These messages sound like: "You shouldn't feel that way," "Don't be scared," or, "There is nothing to be scared of." All of these deny our feeling experience and fail to comfort our inner child. A loving response would be, "Of course you feel scared, (mad, sad, etc.). Any child would. I'm here with you. I'm watching over you and I'll take care of you." **The Higher Self voice only helps, encourages, praises, gives us permission to go ahead, supports our process of individuating, and says "No!" to ways that would harm us.**

Our critical voice may tell us things to do which are appropriate things to do. The instructions may also be incorporated in our mind with reversed intent. For example, we may have received all our instructions as to how to handle being safe in traffic as, "Don't do this and don't do that in order to be safe." We may have heard, "Watch out!" or, "Be careful!" Even if these instructions came as, "Do this to be safe," we most likely habituated out of fear of not doing things right, and therefore, the thinking is part of our defense system. When we re-evaluate information we learned in early years and find it still valid, we only need to switch our intention by deciding to do it as a free choice. Then our inner messages sound like, "I choose to do this and this in order to be safe."

FREE OF BLAME WE SEE GOD.
OUR PURE HEART BRINGS ONLY BLESSINGS.

13

DOING SPIRITUAL WORK

*I tell you the truth, unless you change
and become like little children,
you will never enter the kingdom of heaven.
Therefore, whoever humbles himself like this child
is the greatest in the kingdom of heaven.*
Matthew 18:3

**Heaven is our healed state. We are in heaven when we
return to God after having defended. The time we spend
separated from love is hell. To be in heaven is to be happy.
Only our defensive nature, our identity as an abandoned,
wounded child dies out. In our state of heaven, we are radiantly alive. Heaven is home for the soul.**

The most important element in all healing practices in *Forgiving Is the Only Real Solution to Violence* is the response from
our Higher Self. I have known people to tell or write out their
troubles for what seemed like forever, cry into their pillows for
years, and destroy one relationship after another with anger as a
way of life. What is missing in all of these pictures is the response of a comforter. They hear no voice responding. They all
identify as an abandoned, wounded child.

IN SPIRITUAL WORK WE:

    1. Remember early scenes - where we first had
       the feelings we are having now and re-
       stricted in response. (If I'm 40 years old, I

may be healing an event that took place
when I was 39. In this case, "child" means
who I was at 39 when my feeling nature
was overwhelmed by some life event. Be
sure to look for an earlier life scene with
the same pattern, also.)
2. Walk into each as the person we are now.
3. Meet the needs of our child we were then
from our Higher Self.
4. Remove our child from the scene.
5. Bring our child home with us - integrate the
separated part into our present awareness
of ourselves.

ESSENTIAL STEPS IN HEALING EARLY SCENES:

1. Recognize the need to heal.
2. Believe we can heal.
3. Decide to do it.
4. Remember the scene with only one goal -
freeing our child.
5. Recognize decisions made by our child that
limit.
6. Redecide as a thinking/feeling person.
7. Relate learnings to a current situation.

1. Recognizing the need to heal -
Life presents one problem situation after another.
We do not have fewer problems as we grow, we simply
learn to solve them faster and with greater ease. When
we are free of defensive limitations, we have enough options to respond to situations in ways that eliminate
problems. **The need to do spiritual work is signaled
by a restriction in our ability to solve a problem.**

2. Believing we can heal -
**Only in practicing forgiveness do we realize the
power we have.**

3. Deciding to do it -

The natural process of growth is the solving of one problem situation after another. Truly solving a problem situation means resolving it harmlessly. **Any solution that brings more harm is not a real solution.**

We must learn to discern whether problems that follow our actions come from being harmful, or whether they come as part of the natural process of growth. Life itself brings us a new challenge as we solve the one at hand. There have been times when I have enjoyed receiving a new problem or challenge in my life because I recognized this as a sign that I had resolved the previous one that had been heavy on my heart.

We must learn to discern where we are being harmful and where others are making us wrong for growing. Every step in our growth invites those around us to grow with us. Those not willing to grow seek to restrict our growth. They are threatened by us, call us hurtful, are angry with us for changing, and blame us for their discomfort.

Here are some examples of harmless changes we may make to which others often claim we are being harmful:

♦ no longer giving in to their demands

♦ no longer sacrificing for them

♦ no longer denying and going along with nonsense

♦ no longer staying silent about their harmfulness

♦ no longer doing their work for them as in delivering messages they are afraid to deliver

♦ no longer taking responsibility (blame) for their actions

♦ no longer listening to unending complaints about others

♦ no longer listening to stories about "poor me"

♦ no longer cleaning up their messes

♦ no longer picking up their debts

♦ no longer doing anything for them that they are refusing to do for themselves

♦ no longer doing for others what intuitively feels wrong

♦ no longer attending family gatherings which reenact family battles

♦ no longer associating with institutions that deny our soul

4. Remembering the scene with only one goal - freeing our child -

Healing only takes place when we forgive, which is to correct our desire to blame and harm. The wounded part of us never wants to pardon or excuse the one we see as harming or ignoring us. ("Of course!") At the same time, our soul which is our deepest nature always wants to love and be loved. **As Beloved, we want to see a protector whom we love, know that this protector sees we are hurting, have that protector hear and believe what we say, receive care for our feelings, and receive help out of the situation.**

5. Recognizing decisions made by our child that limit -

The question we need to answer is, "What did I decide when I experienced myself without a caring person in my early scene?" **In defending, we decide both what *not to do* and *what to do.*** These decisions set in motion processes which further compound. The earlier

98

we make them in our life the more broadly they affect our life.

For example, I'm in a scene where no one seems to see what I see, say what I say (or want to say), feel what I feel, or want what I want. I decide I am wrong to see what I see, wrong to feel what I feel, wrong to want what I want, and wrong to say what I see, feel, and want. I decide I am a misfit and don't trust myself. I hold back my natural loving expression in all kinds of ways. So, I *decide not to* express my natural self.

Then I *decide to* get attention or safety by doing things like acting as others act, withdrawing to silence, escaping to fantasy, getting sick, actively disrupting, or passively disrupting by leaving omissions. Behaviors we choose when we believe no love is available are substitutes for what we truly want. They distract us from our original terrifying circumstance. Distractions that serve as substitutes include: acting nice, acting pitiable, acting strong, being a martyr, selling our body, stealing, and abusing food and substances to try to get love. Anything that demands attention by causing disturbance falls into this category including doing nothing, if it is done to disrupt. Anything that scares, maddens, provokes grief, or lures attention is a substitute. **Our only true want as a soul is to love and be loved for who we truly are as we live our life.**

6. Redeciding now as a thinking/feeling person -
Our being present for our inner child allows us (as the child) to receive the loving response we need. This response empowers us. We do not need to engage in any battle with another person. As the child, we are free to take the hand of our own grown-up and leave the scene.

Yesterday the pain in my back, which I heal as I write, began to scream at me. I realized my inner child was screaming. The early scene that came to mind was my dad supposedly taking care of me and my siblings, all preschoolers, to give my mother a rest. We were to be quiet to please both of them. As we three young ones sat in front of the fireplace, he made it look to us like he was going to set the house on fire. Meanwhile, the game was that he would give a penny to the last one to scream. I was usually the first to scream. I was trapped between giving a natural response of alarm to try to save myself from the fire, and trying to save myself by being quiet to please him. My screams were met with his loud guffaws. "Cruel!" "Cruel!" I named it for her to validate her experience and took her from the scene. I know that anything except brief anger at him would only keep her stuck in the scene, so I invite her to give and receive love now with me which is what she wanted then and can now have. I appreciate her natural signals of alarm that I use to protect myself from danger. I will do nothing to encourage her to deny them.

The pains of our body are from scenes in our mind that are incomplete. They cry out to us to heal. We heal by thinking of them as our inner child crying out. When we say I hurt, rather than my body hurts, we have turned our attention to ourselves rather than our body. This is the moment we need to respond as our Higher Self.

7. Relating learnings to a current situation -

The fact that an early scene has come to our mind means that we are ready to heal. This relates to some current problem in our life and the Holy Spirit re-members that we restricted and what the circumstances were at the time. Life is truly wonderful! We need only learn to appreciate it and cooperate with it to be truly happy, productive, and kind people.

I am called to give the message of *Forgiving Is the Only Real Solution to Violence* to the world. The message is contrary to the world's belief that violence is the solu-tion to all our past and current hurts. I heal blame stored in my body, I heal how I learned to be powerless when others were violent. I free myself from believing I am a misfit because I do not maintain silence in the face of harmfulness. I free myself to say what I feel in my heart and know to be true at the level of my soul. **I am on earth to love and be loved.**

WHEN DOING SPIRITUAL WORK REMEMBER:

If you are concerned about being able to handle memories coming up, seek help from a professional. A truly helpful professional practices forgiveness and will help you see that you have a grown-up part of you to attend your emerging child. Being with them will inspire you to respond to your inner child kindly, gently, or firmly if necessary. If the professional's approach is such that you must continue to see them regularly to tell them your troubles, they are not healthy themselves.

Doing spiritual work is similar to bringing bad dreams to completion by imagining safe endings. Since you are doing spiritual work in your imagination, you can bring into your mental picture all the forces you need to help you. If a person in a scene you are healing is overpowering you, bring into your picture someone to help you. Holy forces include God, Jesus Christ, Mary, a Guardian Angel, etc., or bring in a person like a grandparent (who is living or not). Imagine any equipment that would help protect you while you do what you need to do to heal the scene. Equipment might include a Plexiglas shield between you and your offender, a pink bubble to surround you, a moat, or radar to alert you to danger of someone coming toward you.

There are those who suggest setting up battle scenes in visualization to deal with those things that frighten us including diseases such as cancer. To do so is to engage with them. The law of life is that anything we antagonize increases because we give energy to it. I believe it is a higher choice to find a way out of any situation without having to fight against anyone or anything. I feel comforted when I hear myself say, "I will no longer be part of this."

Our diseases represent our inner child frozen somewhere in time. Should we set up war against the disease, we may well be setting up war against our inner child. Our diseases appear when and where we have not as yet been loved, so strange as it may seem, loving our diseases is what we need to do.

Many times I find that saying, "This is energy moving," enables energy that I once blocked to begin to flow. This is a statement made from thinking awareness. Otherwise I find myself responding as an abandoned child increasing the symptoms by tensing against them.

EXAMPLES OF FORGIVING:

1. One day I had the sense that a witch loomed in my presence and I was a small child in a box. There was no way that I would come out of the box as long as she was there. Nor was I willing to engage in battle with her. I told my husband about my predicament and he came up with a very creative solution. He said, "Well, old witches retire to Florida." That is all he needed to say. As soon as I saw the witch on the sunny beach, she wilted and disappeared in the sun. Obviously, the witch was a construct of my defense system, images of "bad mother" too painful to entertain as a child. In one instant, I was free of them. Notice that the problem was solved by bringing in light!

2. I once went back to the most terrifying scene of my childhood to see my inner child, age two, in a coma from having a very high fever with pneumonia. Over a period of weeks, I returned to this scene. At first, I imagined myself sitting at the bedside stroking and talking to her. Soon I was holding her on my lap. Then I began taking her out to play. One day I told her to meet me under a tree on a grassy knoll. When the time seemed right, I asked her to come with me and she has been an integrated part of me since.

I had actually experienced this coma as a child. As an experience at the emotional level, I had deadened massive amounts of feeling I was not able to handle during the illness and hospitalization. Though I had physically wakened from the coma, it was not until I was in my late thirties that I had reached the maturity to heal the feelings. [Note: If I were doing this today I might bring her immediately to live with me. At the time, the six week process worked to heal the scene.]

3. Some years later while doing a serious study of food, I began to feel paranoia. I felt terror, believing I could not trust grocery stores and restaurants to provide safe food for me. I believed they didn't care if I lived or died. There is reason to be concerned about the production and processing of food for public consumption. However, my feelings were totally out of line since I am able to discern and select safe food for myself.

I had help from a counselor to follow this feeling back in time and found myself in the same hospital scene. I began to panic as the memory came to my awareness. I remembered being served food laced with something awful tasting (sulfa) and at the time I was sure those feeding me were poisoning me. I probably believed they were the ones making me sick!

To heal this scene in my mind, I brought in my Higher Self and two friends that I know as intuitive. I had them surround my bed. I immediately felt calm because I believed that no one would get by the intuition of all three of us to trick me with poison. In bringing in reinforcement for my intuition the paranoia left immediately.

When I was two years old, those feeding me ignored my intuitive sense that sought to protect me. I felt powerless to get them to hear me and stop what I experienced as dangerous to me. I didn't understand at the time that they were seeking to save my life.

Our intuition is connected to God. While deadened, my intuition was asleep. As I wakened from this scene of terror, I started trusting my intuition and abiding by its messages even if others didn't see or experience what I saw and experienced. Trusting my intuition has enabled me to see all the reversals necessary to forgive. I share this with you in *Forgiving Is the Only Real Solution to Violence.*

**WHEN HEALED YOU ARE IN HEAVEN.
TO BE IN HEAVEN IS TO BE HAPPY.**

14

NURTURING OUR INNER CHILD

...whoever lives by the truth
comes into the light,
so that it may be seen plainly
that what he has done
has been done through God.
John 3:21

WHAT IS NURTURING?

To nurture is to nourish, or to give and receive that which feeds our soul. Living spiritually is characterized by nurturing. Nurturing is an attitude, a stance we hold toward something. Our defensive stance is that there is no love available for us so we don't see it even when it is there. Our nurturing stance is that love is freely available to us for the asking. We ask by releasing our defensive stance and accepting a receptive stance which welcomes love. *When we are aligned with God, we only want to receive and give that which assists, protects, and furthers life.* Nurturing is done through our nature that aligns with God as opposed to our nature that aligns with defenses.

We are nurturing when we see the child in every person, the one who only wants to love and be loved. We include our own inner child in this. Holding a nurturing stance and attitude toward our inner child means we are ready and willing to listen and respond to our feelings throughout the day. **We can nurture ourselves no matter where we are just as we can criticize ourselves and others wherever we are.** Nurturing is a choice we make and without making this choice, we automatically use our mind to think critically and project blame.

Nurturing is gentle, not weak. Nurturing extends light and love firmly and directly in a way that fosters trust. Being free of illusion, it zeros in on real needs like a gentle laser. The directness of gentleness has no harmful intent and in its presence we feel safe. It is the safety of a nurturing environment for which we all long. Safety is essential to grow our soul.

Nurturing our inner child is something that is simple, meaningful, powerful, and the only sensible thing to do. It need not "take" time. It is a matter of giving our thoughts a new direction. That time which we would ordinarily have spent criticizing, worrying, hassling, and doubting ourselves is time we "give" ourselves lovingly. We use our time to praise, give information, repeat affirmations, and talk to ourselves about the reasons we are taking new directions. I hear people say that time they spend driving is wasted time. I find this to be a wonderful time to "give" nurturing to myself rather than criticize other drivers.

In Chapter 5 of my first book, *Sharing the Course,* there is a lengthy description of five healing methods, all of which join our Higher Self and inner child. Along with each is a list of problems you might have in using the technique and what to do about them. In *Forgiving Is the Only Real Solution to Violence,* I use various techniques. For additional examples and deeper understanding than you find here, please consult *Sharing the Course.*

A MASK OF NURTURING

There is a masquerade of nurturing which quite commonly is misnamed as nurturing. People who identify as unloved victims switch from this one-down position to that of one-up rescuers. From this position, they feel more powerful and are bent on helping everyone else heal to avoid feeling unhealed feelings. Rescuers have only switched to another stance on the defensive or dark side of existence. These people are the unhealed healers who hide from themselves that they have not truly healed themselves. We find this mask everywhere we find people helping people including in parenting and in all professions that serve people.

The deeds in these false representations of care are not of God, but of a wounded child acting like a helper. The most obvious sign of this is the stance, "I want to help *others* and learn more and more ways to help *others*." This masquerade becomes a problem in Twelve Step programs when people focus on helping others at the neglect of doing their own spiritual work. Switching from one-down to one-up means we have simply switched to another role in an addiction pattern. We have not forgiven to release the pattern of addiction.

Often this masquerade is carried out "in the name of Jesus" or as having been "born again." Those who live in a healing, forgiving way do not need to verbally and publicly proclaim their rebirth. Their attitude reflects their growth. We feel safe and good when we are with people who forgive and nurture themselves. Their behaviors indicate that they have learned to love themselves and we feel inspired by the way they live. Above all we do not sense that we have to change to please them. Those who have not healed themselves are always trying to change us and believe they are helping us by doing so. We experience this as being made wrong and as never being good enough (in their eyes).

SELECTING NURTURING NAMES

I suggest you have a name for your inner child to use while nurturing yourself. Usually this is your own name as you were called as a child. You also need an identity for the grown-up you. Over the years I have thought of NP, Nurturing Parent, as my grown-up self and LN, Little Nancy, as my young self. I am ever more comfortable with HS as Higher Self since it also represents Holy Spirit to me. As I use HS I continue to deepen my appreciation of the gift of the Holy Spirit in my life. Do what feels best for you. The names you use need only be terms of endearment or something you say with affection and gratitude.

WAYS TO NURTURE

One way or another, we use our imagination to nurture our inner child. Sometimes we nurture ourselves simply by picturing ourselves at some young age and making the picture a loving experience. This age might change in our mind from moment to moment. Our child's emotions change just as quickly. We simply connect with our inner child and extend the most loving words and actions we can imagine.

For example, I had a nagging feeling for several days and finally figured out what was causing it. From spending long days at the computer writing this book and then reading what I printed out, my eyes had taken on a fixed stare. My delightful child informed me that my eyes wanted to dance. After hearing this message, I became aware that I was going from staring at the computer to staring at the car in front of me while driving. I also had a fixed stare as I talked with people. Then I went to dance class and realized I had a fixed stare on the leader. So I decided to let my eyes dance. I spent the rest of dance class in conversation with Little Nancy. It went something like this:

HS- You don't have to watch her. You can just listen to what she says and let your eyes dance.
LN- I like to watch my hands as I dance.
HS- Yes, that is fun.
LN- Sometimes I like to look at my hand and then the leader and let my eyes look close and far.
HS- That's very good, Nancy.
LN- Oh! I'm surprised I didn't get dizzy watching my arms make those big circles.
HS- Well you didn't.
LN- I wonder if anyone is watching my eyes dance. I probably look really funny.
HS- You probably do. They are probably staring at the leader.
LN- This sure feels good. Whoops, I just got off rhythm with my legs. It is hard to think about what my legs are doing, how I'm breathing, and what my eyes are doing.

HS- Yes, I know. It is okay if you get off rhythm now
and then. It is rather important to remember to
breathe! Let your focus go from one thing to another. That will be refreshing, too. When we focus too hard on any one thing it is just like
staring at the computer.

**Another way to nurture ourselves is to use a doll, stuffed
animal, or even a favorite pillow to represent our inner child
giving us something to hold while we talk.** I have known people to resist this for years and then be truly touched upon accepting it as valid for themselves. I believe we act tough and feel
fragile until we accept this tender part of ourselves and sustain it
with strength of awareness.

**Another way to nurture ourselves is to use a journal and
write out a two-part dialog speaking from both voices.** Because we receive an immediate response from our Higher Self as
we speak, this technique comforts. We say from our inner child
what we have waited for someone to hear, and know right away
that we have been heard. Some people make this technique more
powerful by using different hands to write from each voice. Use
your dominant hand for your grown-up voice and your non-
dominant hand for your inner child. Dialogs would be similar to
those you have already read in this book and those in following
chapters.

**Another way to nurture ourselves is to use a mirror, con-
sider ourselves as the grown-up and the reflection in the mirror as our inner child.** We hold a dialog speaking from both
voices. There is more about this in Chapter 15.

THE LAW OF NURTURING

Love heals. This is the law of life. As we begin to nurture
ourselves, we give the signal to God, or the Holy Spirit part of
ourselves, that we are ready to stop blaming and to receive love.
Then the scenes that we placed on hold start coming to memory
for us to heal. Each scene that comes to mind tells us where we
are to take the hand of our inner child.

Love and prayer work the same. When we pray, things begin to break down that do not fit with that which we are inviting into our life. Making a nurturing connection with our inner child is much the same. As soon as we begin to connect with our child, we start remembering hurts from our past. Life may seem like it is getting worse. This is not true, however. Our inner child gains hope of receiving love and we are simply being shown where to extend love. The continuous process of connecting with our inner child in early scenes is our spiritual growth.

For example, I make a flyer. I take a look at it and instead of my usual way of criticizing myself, I follow my urge to say, "Good job, Nancy!" I no sooner do this than I feel angry. In receiving this longed-for praise from myself, I tap into memories of times when I received criticism instead of praise. I had repressed both my hurt and the anger that covered it.

So, now that I feel angry, I need to continue to be there in my responses. I talk to Little Nancy. "Of course you feel angry. It is very hurtful to not receive praise for things you do. I understand how you would want to change others with your anger to try to get praise from them. It doesn't work, however. I have a better way for you. You and I are together now and I know the praise you need. I'll give it to you generously. Are you willing to stop blaming those who didn't praise you so you can receive my praise?"

And, of course, this is the critical question. Do we want to continue to blame for our hurt and try to get others in our past to praise us, or accept inner praise now? For our soul this is a life and death question. It is not that the soul dies. The soul remains dark, non-receptive to light, and non-radiant until we are willing to take in love. We know no happiness with an unlighted soul.

In the natural healing process, we feel our original hurt when we know love is available. My being there for myself with praise was a different voice that provided love not criticism. My new loving response signaled readiness to heal early life scenes where I received criticism and no praise. I anticipate that many scenes with the same pattern will come to mind for me to heal.

The original criticism came from outside myself. Note in this example that I carried on the process as a way of relating to myself for many years after that. So now I must discipline myself to watch for my pattern of criticizing myself and be sure to give praise instead.

Remember that the Holy Spirit aspect of ourselves is God's answer to any void. If we were not praised as a child, we have an aspect of ourselves that knows just what praise we need. We choose whether to speak from the loving voice to ourselves. We choose whether to listen to this voice from our receptive selves. As we praise ourselves, we become attractive to others and they begin to praise us. It is also true that many people praise us before we open to receive it and we bat the praise away believing we do not deserve it.

RECEIVING STORED FEELINGS

Any stored feelings that we allow ourselves to feel and that we receive with love will not last more than moments. One way or another the fact that we have stored our feelings means we believe we are unsafe or wrong to feel them. Therefore, as we begin to receive our feelings we must be alert for ways others made our feelings wrong. Typical discounting statements are: "You shouldn't feel that way," "Don't be scared," "There's nothing to be scared of," and, "If you want to cry I'll give you something to cry about."

Statements that encourage our inner child to reveal feelings to us are: "Of course," "Tell me more about it," "What are your tears saying?" and, "Are you also _____ (another feeling)?"

So often issues come up at times when we are not free to attend them. If this happens to you, simply tell your inner child you are aware that there is a need for you to attend and commit yourself to do your spiritual work at the first possible moment. For example, you start to feel angry. Perhaps you will say to your inner child, "Yes, I know you are angry. I'll see to it that we resolve this before going to bed tonight." Simply acknowledging the feeling means your child will wait for your help. Earn the trust of your inner child by keeping your word. With trust of

111

you, your inner child will learn that you respond to minor signals and will have no need to build anger to the point of rage to get your attention. Where there is anger, look for hurt, scare, and sadness. Scenes usually resolve when we get to tears.

FEAR

When we are faced with an emergency situation and our body responds with a supply of adrenaline, we are grateful for our added strength to handle the emergency. People do remarkable feats under such circumstances. **Most fear comes from our inner child not feeling protected by our Higher Self. Fear which comes from identifying as an abandoned child may go on for years. We were not meant to live with chronic fear.**

It is natural to feel fear when doing something new. We heal when we are mindful that we are both the child with emotions and the Higher Self with abilities to tend the waking child. When these aspects come together, we have courage to solve any problem. With courage, we do what needs to be done and receive information in the process that relieves our fear of the unknown.

At the times when we froze scenes, we were experiencing helplessness and terror. So, we often experience a moment or more of helplessness and terror as we release blame in the waking process. If we scare ourselves and brace against release of feelings, we prolong the process. And if we medicate the emerging feelings away, we fail to receive our feelings with love and miss the healing moment. I have found that when I allow my heart to race without telling myself I am going to die, my heart comes to peace within three or four deep breaths. Fear subsides when we say from our Higher Self, "I am here for you now. You are coming alive, not dying."

We know when a healing has taken place by our sigh. The characteristic sigh of relief comes when our inner child knows it is protected by our Higher Self. Be aware of it. When I sigh, I also say, "The crisis is over." Many crises in your life are now over and you haven't said this. Take a few moments to repeat, "Sigh, the crisis is over," giving big sighs as you do it. You will experience a refreshing release of tensions you have held in your body.

ANGER

Anger is the energy of blame, the energy we express to be one-up and scare others into being one-down. It is natural for us to feel angry as a child because we are frustrated by our immature abilities. We are given the ability to be angry so we can demand that others help us. Even so, we may not get the help we need. In addition, we may express anger and be overpowered by people that are bigger and more powerful than we are. For these reasons, and more, we end up believing we are unsafe to express anger and store it instead. So, as part of healing, we deal with the release of stored anger.

By its nature, anger calls us to focus our attention. When our intention is to heal, we give our attention to where we are angry/blaming to see where we have restricted ourselves. We heal the scene at that point. When we are blaming, we are willfully projecting energy outward. We cannot be angry and receive love at the same time. We need to become tender to receive love. The tender emotions of hurt or sadness behind the anger are receptive. We express anger in a healing way to listen to our inner child's hurt and become receptive to love in the process. As we receive love we become happy.

One way to look for repressed anger is to listen to your language. Scenes of anger are also where we use the words "I can't" to instruct our subconscious to continue defending and not become receptive. Therefore, the words "I can't" point the way to scenes that need to be healed. For example, we might say, "I can't trust my boss," "I can't find anyone to date," "I can't tell her anything," "I can't sing," "I can't give a speech," or, "I can't play tennis." All of these have unhealed early scenes behind them. In each case, the "I can't" indicates we choose to continue to secretly hold the scene in mind, and blame rather than heal. In other words, if I say, "I can't write," I secretly hold memories of feeling threatened by criticism or rejection from others at times when I revealed myself in writing in the past. **Change each "I**

113

can't" to "I am now safe to see what I have hidden from myself that I might set myself free."

In the following practices, the goal is to listen for the complaint and hurt of your inner child. Your goal is to expand at
some point where you once restricted and have remained so.
Until you feel your tender emotions and resolve them, you fuel
anger. Unhealed anger cycles to ever greater intensity turned
inward as resentment or outward as hostility. Unhealed anger
becomes the basis for dis-ease and violence.

Here are some safe ways to express anger to heal:

1. Write it out.
    Write it out with as many profanities as you need to
use to release it. Then shred or burn what you wrote.
Do not send or give it to anyone. When you have identified your tender hurts or needs, nurture yourself and
share those tenderly with a nurturing person. Most
people respond to tenderness and are repelled by anger.

2. Scream it out.
    If you are alone, scream or growl. If a cooperative
person is present, tell them you are about to scream.
Maybe they would like to scream with you! Otherwise,
go to your (parked) car or to the woods and let out your
anger with your voice. If need be, scream into a pillow.

3. Pound it out.
    You may do this alone, or with a loving person be-
side you. **The rules are:** You may say anything you
need to say and strike as hard as you need to strike.
You may not hurt yourself, anyone else, or any property
with your anger. Either be alone in the house, or at
least tell others what you are about to do so they are not
frightened. Now, take off any jewelry and watch, loosen
any tight clothing, and remove anything else that might
be in the way when you swing your arms. Kneel on a
pillow beside your bed. Fold your hands palm to palm
so you do not injure your fingers. Put your clasped

hands over your head and bring them down onto the bed with all your strength. Meanwhile, put words with each swing and shout them. Most often I hear things like:

"I hate you!"
"Stop hurting me!"
"Get out of my life!"
"Leave me alone!"
"This is my body!"
"Xxxxxxxx!!!"

You'll know what to say. With your rage spent, you will collapse onto the bed in a comfortable fatigue and cry tender tears. You released the energy of blame and have made yourself tender and receptive to love. It is comforting at this point to fall into the arms of a friend beside you. It is also true that in *deciding* to express anger in this way, and following the above rules, you are using your own Thinking Nature/Higher Self, so you will not feel alone even if no one else is present with you.

There have been times when I was in a place where I was not free to pound. I have both imagined myself pounding on a bed, and have also imagined my little child throwing a royal temper tantrum. I had freeing results with no one knowing what I was seeing in my mind's eye.

You can also imagine yourself doing this technique if your body is such that you would harm yourself (have arthritis, diabetes, cardiovascular disease, etc., or you are a smoker).

4. Sing and cry it out.
Your voice is a powerful healing tool. All feelings naturally heal through vocal expression. Let your body sing what it wants to sing. Make the sounds you want to make. Do not do this AT someone else unless you are imagining their presence.

5. Stomp around.

Inform anyone in your space what you are about to do. Then, CHOOSE to stomp around the room. This is different from stomping around the room or slamming a door to get someone else to come and solve a problem for you. Choosing is having the presence of mind to allow your feeling nature/inner child a safe way to express a feeling as part of your healing process.

6. Break something.

Inform anyone in your space what you are about to do. Then, CHOOSE to break something as a piece of cardboard or a dead tree branch. Tear up an old phone book or a magazine.

7. Throw something.

If you want to throw something, follow all of the above rules for safety.

8. Pull on a towel.

Roll up a towel and pull it horizontally using arms and upper back muscles. Add a scowl and a growl.

9. Kick it out.

a. Kick a soft object like a pillow.

b. Lie on your back on a bed and kick downward one leg at a time with your knees bent. Add your fists, swinging your same side arm and leg together. Turn your head toward the active arm and leg.

c. Stand in a box and fuss when you feel like you have something to fuss about. Protect your feet with shoes. Have a box large enough to swing your legs, and shallow enough to step out easily. If the box is too deep, you may fall forward and hit your head on something or harm your arms as you seek to break your fall. Fuss until you experience a shift of energy. Then take some constructive action.

10. Listen to your body.

Listen for what your body wants to do and find a safe way to do it. **When you are fearful, you want to** *run away,* **or perhaps, scream.** Let yourself go for a run or run in place. Scream as instructed above. If your body is shaking, help energy move by purposefully shaking your arms. If you feel like you want to throw up, a deep scream from the bottom of your belly will release the energy with much less mess!

When you are angry, you want to *attack* **one way or another.** Usually this will be a desire to tell someone off, hit, bite, kick, or strangle. Imagine that someone as being present and tell them off, use any of the methods listed above, or bite a towel, strangle a pillow, etc. (I do not mention guns or other weapons here because I would not consider having them in my presence.) There is always a safe way to express anger.

Now remember to give love and protection to your inner child. That is what your child needed and that is what you were mad about not receiving in the first place. When you heal your inner separation, you will no longer be angry. If you continue to be angry, you are choosing to blame rather than open to love.

SADNESS

One day a client called me because she had just had a "panic attack" while driving. I suggested that she put the phone down and shake her body to help it do what it wanted to do. After doing that, she told me she felt like screaming. I suggested that she put the phone down and scream. After doing this, she said she felt like running away. We had quite a lot of snow on the ground at the time; so I asked if she had a basement. She did, so I suggested that she run in place for a while down there and then call me back. After running, she asked to come to see me. When with me she wept for over three hours.

Under all these other emotions was a genuine grief for her father who was ill with cancer. She had told me earlier that she had no feelings for her father because of the way he had treated her. Her feelings were there. She had denied and masked them all, including her love and longing to be loved by her father.

117

Sadness, being a tender emotion, is often hidden behind anger. And if we have repressed anger, fear will be closest to the surface. Her fear expressed itself in the "panic attack."

When someone is crying defensively to get attention, their energy is irritating and we want to tell them. "Knock it off already!" They are manipulating for us to be their Higher Self. And, believing that we could make them happy, they are blaming us for their unhappiness. It is an invitation to be angry with them and blame them.

Behind all blame is a need to cry. There are always tears at the point of healing. Tears of healing are experienced very differently. They are genuine expressions of our feeling nature when we are touched by love. They take place when we are in touch both with our Higher Self and our inner child, not when we cry alone into our pillow as the abandoned one. Genuine tears call out compassion in others who then naturally move in gently to tend us.

I am sure you have known someone who was anxious when you saw them four years ago, anxious when you saw them two years ago, and you are sure they will be anxious when you see them two years from now. The same pattern exists with anger and sadness. When we are repressing one or more of the complex of fear, anger, and sadness, we get stuck in the others and our feelings do not resolve. The person stuck in anxiety (fear) needs to look for anger and sadness in early scenes. The person stuck in anger needs to look for fear (scare) and sadness in early scenes. And, the person stuck in sadness needs to look for anger and scare in early scenes.

True emotions include peace of mind, a joyful spirit, and the playfulness of a body set free to dance. All else needs to be healed.

OUR MEANS FOR HEALING IS ESTABLISHED BY GOD. FORGIVING BRINGS STORED FEELINGS TO LIGHT.

15

SEEING THE WAY TO LIGHT

Your eye is the lamp of your body.
When your eyes are good,
your whole body also is full of light.
But when they are bad,
your body also is full of darkness.
See to it, then,
that the light within you is not darkness.
Luke 11:34-35

Having good eyes means having spiritual vision. This means seeing (ACKNOWLEDGING) that which is unseen by our body's eyes and only known through understanding. "Aha! I see!" Having good eyes means seeing (UNDERSTANDING) the importance of turning ourselves toward light. Having good eyes means seeing (REALIZING) how to find darkness within. Having good eyes means seeing (KNOWING) that we find meaning in life by looking within and correcting darkness. Having good eyes means seeing (DISCOVERING) ways to heal. Having good eyes means seeing (EXPERIENCING) that which heals. Having good eyes means seeing (BEHOLDING) God. Living a spiritual life means being (RADIATING) light.

We do not need to dig through our past to find things to heal. Our present problems always point the way to restrictions from our past. We need to look at life with spiritual vision. Problems in our current life tell us we restricted in our past. In the next chapter, I include a long list of things around which we make decisions as children. I have done this to help you realize the enormity of things that we as a people have to heal and also to give hope for healing those things that apply to you. It is very possible that we grew up believing that we need to forgive things which were done to us. When we change our thinking to realize that we wake up from times we closed in fear, this adds many more possibilities to feelings we need to heal. **Seeing where we restricted gives us power to release those restrictions.** May the list empower you by helping you realize what you can heal by simply joining your own loving self with your inner child.

SCENES THAT NEED TO BE HEALED COME TO MIND IN MANY WAYS INCLUDING:

a. A situation in our life has the same pattern as an early scene.

Problem situations repeat over and over until we solve the original problem. It is life's way of letting us know we are restricted in our expression and have more to give and receive in life.

For example, someone speaks critically to you and you typically feel hurt, seek to change yourself to prevent further criticism, and avoid the person. One day, instead of seeing yourself as out of line, you realize the other person is out of line. Rather than become hurt, you see how that person hurts and projects out criticism as a call for help. Instead of avoiding them, you respond kindly and firmly from a higher voice within you. Your strength feels reassuring to them and they reveal to you something going on in their life that is troublesome. Now, instead of being one-up and one-down, you relate to one another realizing you both want to love and be loved.

b. A memory seems to come from nowhere.

For example, you suddenly remember the time your mother took you shopping, forgot you were with her, and left the store without you.

c. Something good happens in our life, and early life decisions that don't fit with it come to our awareness to be healed.

For example, one Easter I received deliveries of flowers from three people thanking me for assisting and inspiring them in their growth. I was so touched that I sobbed. I realized that I had thought of flowers as something that were sent to those who were sick or had died. Here I was receiving them for being well and alive. I was being honored as a growing soul!

d. We have a physical symptom.

We've learned to work with symptoms to bring to awareness emotions that we stored. A scene comes to mind as we remember emotional pain. I give examples throughout this book of healing the symptom of pain experienced in my back.

e. We gain awareness from something we read, hear, see, experience, or are told by others.

For example, something you read in this book triggers a memory for you. Perhaps you, too, were subject to trickery by someone in your young years and gained hope for healing your hurts from my examples. I shared them for this reason.

Another example: My husband often shared with me his dream of having a sailboat. For his birthday, I bought him an audio tape of sounds from a sailing trip and was very excited about giving it to him. We decided to play it while relaxing in bed. Instead of relaxing, I went into panic as soon as I heard the first creaking sounds on the tape. Emotionally, I had gone back to an early life fishing trip with my dad. He was fishing off a sunken barge and watching my two year old brother and me at age four while my mother talked with a friend in the car. My brother fell through a porthole. Upon hearing the splash, my dad frantically began looking for him. Fortunately, my brother's coat had hung up on a nail as he fell through the hole and my dad was able to pull him out of the water. It was a terrifying time for all of us. I doubt that any attention was given to my feelings at the time. My parents became angry to defend their fright and I buried my terror. In remembering the scene, I was able to give my little self the care she needed in that scene.

f. A dream brings a memory to our awareness.

For example, I once had a dream in which raccoons were tearing smaller animals apart with their claws and eating them alive. In another scene, chipmunks were nested in a piano with a stash of nuts. This dream encouraged me to look at a situation in my life in which I was feeling eaten alive by someone. I needed to tend the little me represented by the chipmunks safely nested with a supply of nourishment.

g. Body work or a massage may activate a memory.

For example, in *Sharing the Course*, I tell the story of being at a workshop in which participants were leaning knuckles into knots on each other's backs to get us to release pain we had stored in our bodies. As the woman leaned on me, I began to sob. As a result, I released a pattern of holding back gifts I had to give. After that, I gave value to the spiritual work I had done with individuals and groups over the years. I gave my learnings as a gift to the planet in writing the book, *Sharing the Course.*

h. Natural cycles of life bring up issues for us.

I recommend reading *Cycles of Power: A User's Guide To The Seven Seasons of Life* by Pamela Levin. There are many different cycles in life. Thirteen year life cycles can feel quite devastating if we do not understand them. These take place at age thirteen, twenty six, thirty nine, fifty two, sixty five, etc. We predictably feel tender and vulnerable at these times as they bring up issues from the beginning of life. In each cycle, we have another chance to complete scenes still unfinished for each of the years in the previous cycles of our life.

You may experience uncomfortable feelings and not be aware of an early scene. **You need not remember a scene to do heal-**

ing work. Properly attend any feelings that come up. If you feel like crying, let yourself cry. A memory may or may not come to you as you cry. If you feel angry, express your anger in one of the safe ways given in this book. Listen for what your child is angry about and that will probably bring to your awareness an early life pattern. If you feel frightened, your inner child needs to hear your voice. Speak in ways that give comfort to your inner child and listen for responses. Your child will tell you what it needs. Further instructions for doing healing work are given in following chapters.

Know that when you reach peace you have healed what needed to be healed. Otherwise, sit quietly and reflect back to earlier and earlier times in your life when you had the same feelings you are having now and identify an early scene. **Work with the earliest scene that comes to you whether it was the original or not. The pattern, the decisions you made about yourself and others, the responses you gave to others, and the solution that sets you free are the same.**

Our minds process information through visual, auditory, and kinesthetic channels. Visual deals with seeing, auditory deals with hearing, and kinesthetic deals with feeling and movement. Healing techniques use these three modes also. In visual methods, we imagine scenes. In auditory methods, we write dialogs, speak words, and/or use music. In kinesthetic methods, we use breath, touch, and/or body movements to release stored feelings. The more of these modes we combine in a healing practice, the more powerful or deeply we feel the healing.

VISUAL METHOD: USING IMAGINATION TO HEAL EARLY SCENES

1. Close your eyes and allow a scene to unfold in your mind's eye. Include many senses. See what is there including people, actions, and colors; hear sounds and words that are said; smell the people and environment; taste what is there to taste; and feel ways you were touched or movements you made.

Answer the following questions for yourself:
  How old am I in this scene?
  Where am I?
  Who is here with me?
  Who isn't here with me that I want to be with me?
  What is happening?
  What do I feel?
  What do I decide is the best way to take care of myself in
    this scene?

As the grown-up you are now, walk into the scene. **Be aware that you remember everything about this scene, know what you needed as a child, know what your child needs now, know what needs to be said, and know how to meet your child's needs. This is your gift of the Holy Spirit provided for you by God to heal yourself and make yourself whole/holy.** Bring the scene to conclusion. Take your child home to live with you.

The Holy Spirit never leads us to harm another. It tells us to set boundaries; not cooperate with nonsense; say "No" to that which is not right for us; say "Yes" to that which is right for us; to get help we need; to receive what is truly helpful; and, to break any secrecy which maintains our addictions and then be truthful.

Example: Earlier in this book I spoke of having pain in my upper back. As I write I am learning from what I say. One thing I heard is that in defending, we become unaware of our emotional pain. What actually happens is that we put it into our body and then experience and speak of it as our body that hurts. So, for several years, I have been saying, "My back hurts." Yesterday I changed that to, "I hurt." Tears flowed and in my mind I could see myself around three years old screaming with rage. In Chapter 13, I described this scene where my dad was pretending to set the house on fire. Trapped between crying out with fear at the danger of the fire and needing to please my dad by acting brave I was usually first to scream. I gave up hope for his approval in screaming. His laughter at my "weakness" felt wicked.

In my mind, I returned to the scene and let little Nancy know I saw all about this game. I took her out of the scene and brought her to my home now. I told her that I am very safe with fire and that I protect our home. As I watched her freely trip around this space in her pink bunny suit, I felt delight.

2. Sit in front of a mirror. Think of yourself on the chair as being your parent/thinking nature and the reflection in the mirror as being your inner child/feeling nature. Mirror dialog is very powerful because of eye contact. You can actually see facial expressions change as you switch back and forth in dialog. This method combines visual and auditory modes.

Example of mirror dialog:
(HS is Higher Self, LN is Little Nancy)
HS- Hi Nancy!
LN- Hi!
HS- I'm so glad you are living with me now.
LN- (smile)
HS- I know you've waited a long time to know me.
LN- (She now looks and sounds angry.) What took you so long to come for me?
HS- You are angry aren't you?
LN- Yes, I've been hurting a long time.
HS- Do you mean your back has been hurting a long time?
LN- Well that, too. I mean I have been hurting and you've just been thinking about your back. (Hear the blame from the defended child.)
HS- So the real problem was the one back there, back in time.
LN- Yes. Now tell me what took you so long. (More blame.)
HS- Well, little one, I realize that it seems that you were without love for a long time. You've been waiting for your daddy to change and blaming him for not being loving to you. You could not do that and see me here. While you've been focusing on the pain in your back we were separated weren't we. (The Higher Self ignores the blame and both

welcomes the child and gives helpful information.)

LN- Yes

HS- And, little one, I realize that a marvelous process
has been taking place all along. God has made
me perfect at taking care of a little girl hurt just
like you have been. He even inspired me to write
this book so I could come to realizations I needed
to join with you. You must have grown in trust
of me as you realized I understood about little
girls who are hiding and asleep.

LN- Yes, you are very smart. I feel good with you. I
know you won't hurt me like Daddy did. (The
defended child responds to the welcoming spirit
of the Higher Self and opens - releases blame to
receive love now - forgives.)

HS- That's true, indeed. I will only protect and care for
you.

LN- How do I know you won't leave me? (The innocent
child seeks to build trust and befriend the Higher
Self.)

HS- I am part of you and will never leave you. I do need
to tell you something, though. You have a
choice. You can be angry with your daddy and
continue to feel hurt, or you can be with me and
be happy.

LN- I don't want to hurt any more.

HS- Good. Then remember I am here for you.

LN- I want to be happy.

HS- Of course! Are you willing to stop all waiting for
your daddy to change?

LN- I wanted him to love me.

HS- Of course! Only a person who hurts would hurt
you. I'm sure he had hurts in his life that he had
not yet healed.

HS- Are you willing to love him even if he was hurtful to
you?

LN- Well, yes, he was usually loving to me and I do feel
loving toward him.

LN- Now I feel angry with God.

HS- I'm glad you told me that. Tell me more about that.

LN- Well, why did he create a world where people are mean and people hurt?

HS- God created life in such a way that there is a healing force for every wound. Sometimes people are mean. Sometimes we hurt. We also have the ability to heal. You have healed from every injury and sickness you have ever had. You are also to heal from every hurt. I am here to join with you for this purpose so you can be happy.

(I sense a small child wraps her arms around me and snuggles to receive the warm care she has needed. The healing feels complete. Sigh!)

AUDITORY METHOD: USING SPOKEN OR WRITTEN WORDS TO HEAL EARLY SCENES

Example of written dialog:

HS- Nancy, I see your daddy is using one of his tricks. It isn't right.

LN- He scares me.

HS- Yes, of course!

LN- He laughs when I tell him to stop and I feel like I'm bad.

HS- Yes, I know. Nancy, your sense of danger is natural and correct. It is not right for him to violate your sense of danger.

LN- I really feel angry at him for ignoring me.

HS- Yes, of course! Daddies are supposed to protect their little girls and he isn't protecting you.

LN- He makes me feel bad for saying "Stop!"

HS- Yes, I know.

LN- There is no way I can get him to love me. If I say nothing to him I feel so scared and helpless that I cry. Then he laughs. If I scream, he laughs.

HS- Yes, I see. Come with me out of this scene. I love you. I really love you. I will never laugh at your signals of danger. They are so important to me to keep you safe. You are precious. I adore you. I cherish you. I feel wonderful having you with me. You are a delight!

127

We strengthen our healing by imagining the scene and writing out the dialog at the same time. If we hold a doll or stuffed animal to represent our young self while we imagine and write, we use all three modes of processing information.

KINESTHETIC METHOD: USING TOUCH AND MOVEMENT TO HEAL EARLY SCENES

Years ago a counselor encouraged me to express anger at my dad in scenes like this. I am sure that doing so has helped me get to where I am today. I switched from being helpless and activated my silenced voice. Anger is moving energy and feels powerful compared to energy frozen in helplessness. All anger expressed at others is blame used to try to get them to change.

In *Forgiving Is the Only Real Solution to Violence,* I choose to make the very important point that we must not tie ourselves to a scene with anger and blame. In any early scene, there is scare, anger, and sadness. Anger masks the more tender feelings of hurt, fear, and sadness. From our Higher Self, we need to receive all three of these from our child. If our child does not voluntarily offer the information, we need to ask: What are you angry (mad) about? What are you scared about? What are you sad about? It is when we move through anger to our tender feelings that we heal. We stay angry knowingly or unknowingly until we experience ourselves as a feeling person in the care of our Higher Self.

Then, if we do not remove our child from the scene after expressing these feelings, we are still stuck blaming others for not feeling loved. Healing integrates these separated parts of ourselves into present awareness.

Example: I take a pillow that represents Little Nancy and I hold her on my lap. I feel her bouncy spirit when she feels safe in my embrace. She brings a new lightness to my spirit. As I imagine myself holding her, I place my hand on the spot where she has felt pain over the years and say, "Yes I know you have a tender spot. I touch you lovingly to acknowledge the hurt you have experienced. I know you will be free of this physical pain for your life will be good with me. I will watch over you and keep you safe while you play. I am the protective parent you need. I will listen and respond to you when you sense danger. I'll move you to safety. I feel so happy to experience you in my life. Your active spirit delights me."

You may have done much healing around one or more scenes and find that they come back to haunt you. This means that there are even deeper issues and that there is more power to be reclaimed through awareness. You may simply need to return to the scene one more time to bring your child home with you.

**SEE TO IT THAT YOU USE SPIRITUAL VISION
TO SEE YOUR WAY TO LIGHT.**

16

RECEIVING OUR JUSTICE

Whatever you have learned or received
or heard from me, or seen in me --
put it into practice.
And the God of peace will be with you..
Philippians 4:9

Justice is our healed state in which we are loved, safe, and happy. Peace is our Just reward. The Law of Justice is provided for us to fulfill ourselves by forgiving. It is our life task to see to it that we heal ourselves and receive our Justice. We need only stop trying to punish others and accept the means God provided for us to make our life Just.

God's Justice is the opposite of our justice system which sees to punishment of those we deem as having harmed us. God's Justice focuses on our receiving goodness earned by forgiving. No one can stand between us and our Just rewards. We need only be willing to forgive and remove hate from our hearts.

Here is the list I spoke of earlier. These are all circumstances which potentially overwhelm us emotionally and lead us to defend. They may be in our past, and they may be patterns still repeating in our present. Either way, blaming others and waiting for them to change does nothing to bring our goodness to us. **Forgiving heals our past, gives us peace in the present, and sets our future free.**

FORGIVING HEALS TIMES WHEN YOU:

were sad, scared, lonely, helpless, hopeless, confused, frustrated, jealous, envious, disappointed, embarrassed, or believed you were inadequate or stupid

had an angry outburst, had to deal with someone else's angry outburst, listened to your parents fight, wanted someone to die

felt like your best was never good enough, felt like you didn't fit in for any reason, weren't heard by others, were teased or tickled

had problems with food or eating, had discomfort at the dinner table

had problems sleeping, had nightmares, experienced intrusions by people or sounds in the night, had any sleep related disturbances

felt replaced when another child was born into your family, or people moved in with your family

were told of problems related to your birth, were blamed for problems of your mother or father, were told you were a financial burden - "another mouth to feed"

were scared or hurt because you were sick, went to a doctor, dentist, or hospital

were afraid of becoming ill with a disease; or ill from chemical contamination or radiation

were afraid of dying, nearly died, had a death experience; were in an incubator, in a coma, in an iron lung, on a respirator, trapped in a well or auto;

had an incident with a gun or weapon, were involved in a war fell, were injured in any way, saw blood (your own or someone else's)

were embarrassed due to loss of control over any body function including bursting into laughter at a time that seemed inappropriate

were teased for having a habit like sucking your thumb, biting your nails

were scared or harmed by an animal, had a pet get injured or die

had a sick parent, grandparent, sibling or friend; experienced the death of a parent, family member or friend; were blamed for someone's death

had only one parent, were abandoned by a parent, not protected by a parent, harmed by a parent, had a parent leave due to separation or divorce

did not receive, or could not count on financial support from a parent; were rejected, kidnapped, kept separate from a parent or other family members

moved away from a grandparent or playmate, felt hurt when someone close as a grandparent or playmate moved away from you

moved to a new home, city, or country; lived in an area where you did not speak the language

felt rejected, had problems with body size or image, felt excluded for any reason

saw someone injured or dead; experienced something repulsive; believed the same scary thing that happened to someone else might happen to you

saw a parent drunk or drugged, experienced parents fighting while one or both were drunk or drugged; experienced a sibling drunk or drugged had a language difficulty; speaking, hearing, or visual difficulty

had a physical limitation

didn't understand, believed you wouldn't succeed, believed you would be punished

were punished severely or unfairly

were scolded for making a mess, called names, were beat up, punished for getting into something like a home repair job your parents were doing, had a problem with housework

felt overly restricted, smothered, were actually smothered, discouraged rather than helped to achieve, strangled

first went to preschool, school, or a new school; missed the bus, were taunted at the bus stop, taunted on a school bus, humiliated with jokes or mocking songs, were last to be picked for a team, lost lunch money, had school play yard problems

had difficulty reading, failed an exam, didn't make the team, had a problem on a team

went on your first airplane flight; had a problem flight; had scares related to a train trip, bus trip, boat trip

lost something as your wallet or purse, money, bankbook, keys, a bicycle or toy, an important piece of clothing, an instrument, something used in sports or play

broke something valuable to a parent; had problems with a toy, a machine, a project, a haircut

had a major spill which damaged something in the home, damaged an important piece of clothing were left alone for the first time, had a problem while taking care of yourself or siblings, had a problem with the house like plumbing or fire alarm while alone

had a problem with a sitter or caretaker

had to deal with someone in your family being ill, injured or disabled; lived with social stigma due to being poor, being a minority, having lice; were embarrassed by the circumstances or your parents or siblings

had any problem related to church or religious practice

had a problem while shopping

had a problem surrounding giving and receiving of gifts, a holiday celebration, a family gathering,

fought with a sibling or another child

had a problem with a project or creation: were criticized for your creation, it broke, someone took it

did good deeds and they were not noticed, contributions were not appreciated

had people take credit for things you made or did

were hit by a car; had an accident on a bike or other wheeled vehicle; were in an accident in an automobile, boat or other vehicle; were in a home fire; had an incident with water, perhaps a near drowning

were involved in a home fire: fireplace, stove, furnace, water heater, appliance

were involved in an earthquake, brush fire, flood, sand storm, tornado, hurricane, volcano

had a problem from excess cold, snow, ice; heat, drought

had an incident related to the mail or newspaper delivery

were made wrong for saying what you saw, wanting what you wanted

were harmed by someone being violent, had your property vandalized or harmed in some way

were frightened by something you did by your own choice: took drugs, drove a car without an experienced driver with you, were involved in a robbery or shoplifted, vandalized something

were caught in the act of disobedience, did something malicious and hurt people or property

chose to sneak; lied, were lied to, deceived, tricked, had promises made to you that were broken

stole something or someone stole from you, were unfairly accused

got into someone else's business, someone intruded into your space, were scolded for walking in on a parent in bed or the bathroom

had an incident related to camp, or camping, had a problem on a vacation or trip

were touched, fondled or molested by a woman, man, or another child; experienced incest, rape

had menstrual or sexual problems, were scolded for masturbating or touching private parts, someone exposed themselves to you or undressed you

were mistreated due to homosexuality

had an unwanted pregnancy, abortion, child out of wedlock

were involved with the police, detention home, or prison; your parents or siblings were similarly involved

lived through traumas of your parents as losing a job, being evicted, having a car stolen, going bankrupt, losing a parent

had to be the grown-up for your parent

first baby-sat, took your first job

had some disaster because you didn't have the information you needed, failed at your first attempt to do something like cooking or laundry

had a problem driving

had a problem at work

didn't have enough of something you needed

were unable to fulfill your heart's desire, no one would listen or help

were told you were just like someone else who was not liked

had an incident around a contest, a stage performance, a recital of any kind

had to do something that was not right for you

felt cheated or cheated on, were denied praise or money owed to you, or you withheld praise or payment due to others

were suicidal or experienced the suicide of someone else

The unforgiving either avoid us when we hurt because they do not want to feel their own feelings, or they make us wrong for feeling. Sometimes their making us wrong shows up in attempts to fix us. People who are forgiving become beacons of light for us as we heal. They are those who have healed themselves and know peace. They have compassion for us in our healing process. They stick by us for they are not afraid to feel their own feelings. They maintain hope for our healing.

When we truly accept that every incident in our past is healed through forgiving, there is no reason for us to whine about our lives. When looking to others for help, we need to be honest as to whether we are truly wanting support for our healing. Often what we are really doing is seeking validation for our blame. Conversations can go on for hours while we say, "Ain't it awful (what *they* are doing)." When we only want others to listen to our troubles, we are being abusive. As listeners, we need to learn to say "No" to this abuse from others.

As we heal, we become beacons of light for others willing to forgive. We extend compassion and stick by them because we are no longer afraid to feel our feelings or to give genuine responses. We allow others their healing process without having to intercede and control them. We extend hope to the world for finding peace.

PEACE IS YOUR JUSTICE.
PEACE COMES FROM SPIRITUAL PRACTICE.

17

EXPANDING PRACTICE

You are the light of the world....
let your light shine before men,
that they may see your good deeds
and praise your father in heaven.
Matthew 5:16

For years I worked with my inner child giving her the loving parenting she needed. It was much later that I learned the spiritual significance of what I was doing. At that point, I saw that I was not just tending pain but also healing my separation from God. I have included some of the practices I use. These practices may seem simplistic. However, as we practice them we learn the power of them. I encourage you to use your creativity to find methods that are right for you.

We need not know WHY we do something that is a problem to us. We only need to see THAT we do it to make necessary changes. Therefore, the question, "What am I doing?" is more useful than, "Why am I doing this? The latter often serves as an excuse to continue a harmful pattern. We believe we will stop doing something after we know why we do it. In choosing to heal, our original reason for turning to darkness comes to our awareness when we turn to light. In other words, if I smoke, I do not need to wait for an answer as to why I smoke. If I stop smoking, the feelings that I repress by smoking will come to my awareness. They tell me what I need to heal. I do not just stop smoking. I heal my feelings denied by smoking. The same is true of every addiction.

A. DEFINING A PROBLEM

1. "My Problem Is"

This sounds simple and it is not because we are used to defining problems with blame of others. Take any problem situation and define it starting with the simple statement, "My problem is_____." When you have properly defined a problem, the solution is within that definition. You will be able to solve the problem by making a change in your own behavior. We err on the side of putting another person between ourselves and the solution. As long as we define our problem as requiring someone else to change, we are justifying blame of them rather than empowering ourselves to solve our problem. Define until the problem requires only you to change. Know that when you change, you automatically call for a new response from others.

Example:

My problem is that she just says she is sick and cops out on things.

My problem is that she doesn't care about my feelings.

My problem is that she thinks because she is sick that I should have pity or sympathy for her and not complain.

My problem is that I tell myself I am wrong to fuss because she is sick.

My problem is that I feel helpless when I have no say about our plans changing.

My problem is that I'm angry with her when she gets sick and we have to change our plans.

My problem is that I'm not receptive to her being tender and honest with me about her scares.

My problem is that I have not asked or listened to her feelings.

My problem is that I use blame of her to avoid feeling my own tender feelings.

My problem is that I have not shared my tender feelings with her.

2. Think Structure

This structure published by Pam Levin in *Becoming the Way We Are* helps us start with a feeling as a symptom and see our self-defeating defensive pattern in a way that we can then reverse it to fulfill our heart's desire.

I am feeling **(1)** _____
because I think that if I (behavior I initiate)
(2) _____
I will be (unhealthy Parental response) **(3)** _____
instead of (healthy Parental response) **(4)** _____
so I (problem justifying behaviors, games)
(5) _____ .

On the **first line** we place some feeling that is uncomfortable to us. The **second line** is what we would truly like to be, do, or have. It is the one that we have denied ourselves, or restricted due to fear from having received something other than a loving response to situations when young. It would be our natural way of being that we gave up to defend when we experienced no comforter there for us in any early life scene. Next we identify what we anticipate as a response to our natural way of being. The underlying belief to any response on the **third line** is, "and I will die." I believe I will be unloved, abandoned, harmed one way or another - and die as a result. This is our child view of scenes during our time of physical dependence on a parent. On the **fourth line** we are identifying the parental response that would be the natural loving response. The **fifth line** problem justifying behaviors include all the things we do while defended. These behaviors keep us from doing our natural behaviors which we believe would lead to our death.

When properly defined, all of our steps for reversal become clear. We need to deny line **(3)**, affirm line **(4)**, do line **(2)**, and stop all we do on line **(5)**. Then our feeling on line **(1)** goes away. This reversal includes identifying our problem belief and its correction, our desire and its substitute, and our ineffective behaviors and their effective opposite. A problem identified by a feeling is solved by changing the whole pattern.

Here is a typical problem situation presented to me by clients. I have defined it using this structure:

(1) I am feeling scared.

(2) because I think that if I open to a relationship with a man/woman

(3) I will be rejected

(4) instead of accepted and loved

(5) so I avoid men/women, tell myself all the things that are wrong with me or with them, tell myself there is no one for me, give value to statistics (tell myself there aren't enough to go around), act like I don't want a relationship, make excuses, lie to cover my scare, refuse dates, find fault with them, blame them, blame my parents, blame society, blame God - REJECT MY HEART'S DESIRE!

The solution:

Deny line **(3),** "I no longer need to believe I will be rejected by a man/woman in a relationship (and die because of it)."

Affirm line **(4),** "I accept my heart's desire as valid for me." "I accept and love myself." "I reach out to accept and love others." "I am acceptable and lovable." "I accept love from others." "I see that others are loving to me."

Do line **(2),** which is to open to the relationship your heart desires.

Stop line **(5),** which is rejecting your heart's desire. Stop avoiding possible relationships. Stop all the self-negating and other-negating inner chatter. Forget statistics! You are only looking for one significant other. There are millions of people in the world. Extend yourself truthfully to others. It is the most natural thing in the world to have a mate who is also your best friend and companion. There is no need to be ashamed of this desire or announcing your desire to the world. Align your behavior with what you DO want. Say "yes" even if scared. Hopefully, you've learned enough about blame by now to let that go and choose a higher way.

If you identify with this problem, my greatest wish for you is that you find another teddy-toting person who accepts and loves their inner child. They will also accept and love yours.

B. EXPANDING AWARENESS

1. "I Accept"

To accept is to SEE. When defended, we always perceive something as being there that is not there, and do not see something that is there. In other words, **when blaming we always perceive the other as being at fault for pain from our separation, and we do not see God's healing response of the Holy Spirit which enables us to heal our separation. Accepting corrects this.** To accept does not mean we have to like what we see. It means we are willing to see what is there. Because we can say, "I accept that _____ is unacceptable to me," and continue right on, this exercise has a free flow to it which enables us to expand our thinking. **To expand our thinking is to grow in love.**

Example:
I accept that my dad played tricks on me.
I accept that it is **unacceptable** now for anyone to play tricks on me.
I accept that I felt frightened when my dad did it.
I accept that I felt helpless as a child.
I accept that feeling helpless now is **unacceptable** to me.
I accept that he failed to protect me at the time.
I accept that any anger I expressed didn't change him.
I accept that my mother was not able to stop him.
I accept that I froze my feelings.
I accept that to freeze my feelings now is **unacceptable** to me.
I accept that I lived through my childhood.

I accept that I have many skills to tend my feelings now.

I accept that it is my spiritual work to redeem my inner child.

I accept that it is cruel, harmful, and violent for a parent to betray trust of a child.

I accept that I betrayed myself by blaming all these years, even if unknowingly.

I accept that I stored feelings in my body that have caused me physical pain.

I accept that I betrayed myself by keeping them stored so long.

I accept that my body heals as I get in touch with my feelings.

I accept that I am a master at healing.

I accept that my body is healthy.

I accept that my joy is complete.

2. Flushing with an Affirmation

One way to find out where we are still holding blame is to repeat an affirmative statement and see what *"Yes, but"* thoughts come to our awareness when we write it (or speak it). **Becoming aware of resistance allows us to clear it.**

Example:
I trust myself to remember that when my body hurts, I am denying feelings.
Yes, but I might forget.

I trust myself to remember that when my body hurts, I am denying feelings.
Yes, but I have said so many times that my back hurts.

I trust myself to remember that when my body hurts, I am denying feelings.
Yes, but that doesn't mean I will know what the feelings are.

I trust myself to remember that when my body hurts, I
    am denying feelings.
Yes, but I might despair of figuring out what the feel-
ings are and of solving the problem.

I trust myself to remember that when my body hurts, I
    am denying feelings.
Yes, but I still think of my body becoming crippled in
some way.

I trust myself to remember that when my body hurts, I
    am denying feelings.
Yes, but I'm afraid of becoming helpless. I have to al-
ways be strong enough to take care of myself be-
cause I do not trust my parents to take care of me.

Wow! Notice the identity as a child here that denies all that
I am now. Truth is that I have all the options I need to procure
any assistance I need if for any reason I should need help. I do
not need to fatigue myself by holding muscular tension as a
way of trying to be strong. It is this tensing that creates the
conditions that bring on the belief that I might become crippled.

**In the process of doing any spiritual practice, we sense
completion when a new and freeing thought brings us a
sense of release, safety, and joy.** The last thought provided
insight that set me free.

3. "What if"
    **The defended child asks many "What if" questions to
find out if it is safe to release resistance.** Therefore, it is very
important that we respond with the highest information we
have available to us. We invite our inner child to waken by
making it feel safe. Write each "What if" down and answer it.
**Perhaps the fact that you respond is more significant than
the actual information you give! Your inner child is really
asking, "Is there someone there who will see my problem,
take it/me seriously, and take care of me if something happens?"**

Example:

Child- What if the pain in my back comes back?

HS-   I will remember that it is you that is hurting and I will ask you where you hurt.

Child- What if I don't know?

HS-   I will ask you what you are angry about. I will ask you what you are scared about. And, I will ask you what you are sad about. That may help you figure out where you hurt.

Child- What if I still can't figure it out?

HS-   I will stay mindful that you hurt and I will be tender and kind to you.

Child- What if I publish this book and then people ask about my back and it is worse rather than better? They will think I don't know what I'm talking about in this book.

HS-   Nancy, the same wonderful force that led you to write this book and share this information with others is seeking at every moment to help you waken, heal, and be happy. I trust that force. It has us talking, doesn't it. That is all that needs to take place for you to heal.

Child- Oh, that's right. (Sigh! I experience an energy shift as my thoughts go from fear to loving union.)

4. Holding Grievances

Complaints are grievances and always include blame. Complaining is a pattern carried over from childhood in which we place a demand on others to figure out what we need and meet our need for us. When we have a grievance, it lets us know we either have a need that we have not yet identified, or we have a need to which we are not yet giving a proper response. Either way, we need to change ourselves. **We look inward to define both our need and the appropriate response to resolve it.**

There are many things that are not right and it is important for us to see them and speak up about them. Complaining is not a powerful way to bring change. Its intent is to make the other hurt. When our intent is truly to bring change, we remove this desire to hurt others and ask directly for what we want. Sometimes we need to give information honestly regarding what we see as not right. Many times things are the way they are because no one has yet seen a better way. **If you are fortunate enough to see a better way, share it with no intent to make others wrong.**

Example:

This is how one of my *inner dialog* complaining sessions sounded related to the pain in my back. I am blaming my husband. Notice how he is getting the bad rap when at the time I was not aware of my need to face feelings from my past and free my inner child. Notice also that I am blaming a man for the pain in my back. That was an important clue that I missed. I now know that neither he nor my dad is responsible for the pain that has resulted from my repressing emotion and storing it in my body. **The solution required only that I change my ways.**

"You don't even know my back is hurting."
"You don't even care if my back is hurting."
"I feel like screaming and you sit there reading
    the paper."
"If only you'd rub my back I'd be okay."

Now, the next problem arises. When we stop complaining and change our complaint to a request, we tend to ask for help to meet our need while we still define it defensively. In this example, I would request that he rub my hurting back. Therefore, I am still denying myself as a person who hurts and has stored emotional pain in my body.

A proper request would be to ask him to sit with me and listen as I talk about what is hurting me. Ideally, he would ask key questions like: *"What are you angry about?"* *"What are you scared about?"* *"Where do you hurt in your life?"* *"What are you sad about?"* *"What do you really want?"* and, *"How can I help you?"*

147

Another example:

This is how another *inner dialog* complaining session sounded. This was the one that led to my realizing that I had fixed my eyes in a stare from working long hours at a computer. My first tendency was to blame my husband. I didn't mind blaming the book. I was even willing to blame God for the weather! **The solution required only that I change my ways.**

> "It's been three months since I've been out in the sun."
>
> "It's been two months since I've seen grass or touched the earth." (We've had record breaking sub-zero temperatures and heavy snows in Cleveland this winter.)
>
> "I need a winter vacation in the sun."
>
> "He never takes initiative to plan vacations."
>
> "If I bring it up he'll brush me aside."
>
> "If it weren't for him!"
>
> "If only I weren't spending all my money getting this book printed."

What I realized later was that I allow my eyes to dance when I am outdoors in the sun. I allow my eyes to dance when I work in the yard and garden. I allow my eyes to dance as I absorb all there is to see in a new place. Therefore, my final conclusion was that I needed to allow my eyes to dance. Where I did this was irrelevant. Dance class worked fine. It was my expanded awareness that set me free to meet my real need.

5. Talking to Symptoms

Our body holds pain until we tell our truth - claim our goodness which is our true identity as Beloved. By talking to our symptoms, we seek to know our truth. This process can be done with any sickness, injury, or accident. They all result from separation from God. When separated, we are blaming and this technique helps us see who it is that we are blaming so we can reverse our intent.

Begin by making a list on the left side of a paper of every-thing you'd like to say to the symptom. Then beside each comment respond as the symptom. Here I speak to the pain I experience in my back. Then I respond as though I am that pain.

To the Symptom	**From the Symptom**
You hurt me.	*Yes, I know.*
You make me feel helpless.	*Do I?*
I've tried everything I know to get you to stop hurting me.	*You know more.*
You make me feel weak.	*You aren't weak. You work non-stop.*
You annoy me.	*I get your attention, don't I?*
You distract me.	*Yes, I know.*
You keep me from being happy.	*If I'm not happy I'm not going to let you be happy.*
You weight me down.	*Do I?*
Why are you there?	*So you doubt yourself.*
What will it take for you to go away?	*Love me.*
What do you want me to do?	*Love me.*
You don't fit with who I am.	*I know, I truly don't. You deserve no pain. You are a wonderful person deserving only the highest of rewards.*

When you complete the two columns ask yourself to whom in your current or past life you would like to make each state-ment. In looking over these statements I see that most of the things I said to the symptom are also things my inner child was saying to her dad in the early scene. Intuitively I believe my dad's defensive intent is revealed in the symptom's statement, "If I'm not happy I'm not going to let you be happy." I also be-lieve that he was demanding intense attention as a substitute for love he needed at the time. I felt compassion for him upon realizing this. Compassion is a switch to the holy from blame which is defensive.

6. SOS

This exercise helps us expand awareness by structuring our thought to include ourselves, the other, and the situation. When blaming, we usually omit ourselves. One way or another, we never see the whole picture. Write until you discover a new piece of information that sets you free.

Self-   My life is very good now.
Other-   My dad's life was very difficult for him.
Situation-When I allow myself to feel the feelings I stored, they dissipate in my higher energies.

Self-   I have no need for pain in my body.
Other-   He hurt all his life and died in pain.
Situation-I took on his projected pain and it became mine to heal. (Where he had not released blame against his parents for not loving him, he tried to get love from me using his defensive behaviors.)

Self-   I've become good at processing pain, my own and that I took in from others.
Other-   I won't be taking in any more from him.
Situation-I need to completely release from deadness any other feelings I have stored that they too might be healed.

Self-   This is my time for joy.
Other-   Daddy, I love you and wish only well for you.
Situation-I see that I have grown spiritually and pass on a higher legacy to future generations.

Self-   I would like for my dad to have shown only love to me.
Other-   He did his best and I am to do the rest.

Situation-I choose to treat myself with loving-
kindness.

Self-   I am tremendously gifted by God, my Father.
Other-   God, my Father fills me with love.
Situation-My life is blessed.

7. Hear Words

Think of some goal you currently hope to make true for yourself. Imagine that your dream has now come true.

What do you say to yourself?
What do you say to others?
What would you like to say to others?
What do you not say? To whom?
Do you celebrate you?
Do others celebrate you?
What do they say to you? To others?
What would you like them to say?
What do they not say? To whom?
Who is unhappy, resentful, jealous, envious?
Do you see how they restrict themselves?
Do you see how you have been restricting yourself?
Do you see who you blame?

Only when you believe you are safe to fulfill your goal will you release your resistance to fulfilling it. This practice helps us see what we fear. Usually, when we hold ourselves back from fulfilling our heart's desires, it is because we believe we will be harmed or rejected.

Know that your blaming keeps you from fulfilling your dream. Be willing to stop blaming. Write yourself a letter of encouragement from your Higher Self with words you need to hear to feel safe to go forward. Know that these words will help you fulfill your dream.

Example:
I picture my back healed and free of all pain. I see myself moving gracefully with ease.

151

To myself I say: "Nancy, you've proven once again that you can heal something you once thought you would have to live with forever."

To others I say: "I no longer have pain in my back. I realized I was hurting and displaced the hurt into my body. I solved the real problem. I've regained flexibility and am delighted with my freedom."

I do not say anything to those who would discredit that love heals and I have the ability to heal my body by forgiving.

I celebrate myself and receive smiles and hugs from others.

To me they say: "What a wonderful, inspiring model you are for us! You bring us hope. We admire and honor the spiritual work you do. We admire you for sharing yourself so personally as a teacher. We are deeply touched as we grow and realize the courage of your journey."

8. Release Debts and Debtors

Those that you blame, you believe owe you something. Usually the same people believe that you owe them something. You only need to release your side of the pattern to be "out of debt." This exercise is to help you recognize those places you are stuck blaming or accepting blame.

When you focus on what others owe you, there is something you say you want. However, the reason you feel deprived is because you have not made the internal correction and are still intent on avoiding - defending. Blaming them is a substitute that keeps the focus off your own fear of receiving and your own need to correct yourself.

If you are not willing to receive what you truly want, avoiding seems safer than receiving. Look for early scenes in which you made the decision to avoid rather than receive. Find the source of sacrifice that set up your state of deprivation.

152

Change that decision to free yourself of debt now. **When you want the answer rather than the substitute you will release the debt and be free to receive that which you truly want.**

Those who blame us have not made their internal correction that would allow them to be/do/have what they say they want. They are distracting from the truth of their situation by directing their focus to us. Remember that when those who blame us are ready for the answer rather than this substitute they, too, will release the debt they hold against us to accept what they truly want. When we are forgiving, we do not hold guilt even when others hold blame toward us.

When we nurture ourselves and bring our own dark guilt to light, we release both our sense that others owe us and that we owe them. We become models for those still too fearful to receive what they truly want. Seeing us safe to receive inspires hope in them. Every person is where they are in the process of developing their soul. We need only see to our own growth. This is a full time job in itself!

To recognize those you hold in debt ask yourself:
Who do I hate?
Who do I believe has failed me?
How do I believe they failed me?
What do I believe they owe me?
What do I hate about myself?
How do I fail myself in the same ways now?
What is it I truly want?
Am I willing to stop blaming (them and myself)?
Am I willing to release my self-defeating patterns?
Am I willing to be/do/have what I truly want now whether they accept me or not?
Am I willing to accept that I cause my own pain until I make this choice?

To recognize those who hold you in debt ask yourself:
Who hates me?
Who believes I failed them?

How do they believe I failed them?
What do they believe I owe them?
What do they hate about themselves?
How do I see them failing themselves?
What is it they truly want?
Am I willing to release guilt (stop taking on fault/debt)?
Am I willing to release my self-defeating patterns (seen as trying to please them, change them, fix them)?
Am I willing to accept their receiving what they truly want?
Am I willing to allow them their pain until they make this choice?

9. Self-Criticism

This exercise enables you to externalize and truly see how you criticize yourself. Only in becoming aware of such patterns are we free to change them.

Write a list of self-criticisms. Now ask yourself:
Do I criticize my body?
Is this to avoid seeing that it is myself as a soul that I do not love?
Do I criticize my body rather than recognize that I believe I am not lovable as a soul?
Who do I blame for that which I criticize about myself?
Who do I believe could not love me?
Do I believe God could not love me?
Am I willing to receive loving messages about my self?

Write a list of loving responses from your Higher Self.

10. Scares and Skills

There are many times in our life when we are scared about things and never release our scares. It is like taking a sudden breath in and forgetting to release it. Doing this deadens our feelings. We become more and more helpless to give appropriate responses to harmfulness. For a big sigh, list down the left side of a paper those times when you have been scared. You might begin with your first memories and work to the present. Then, in the right column, list a skill you now have to take care of yourself should each of these situations arise for you again. My guess is that you will soon see that you no longer need to fear most of those situations. Sigh, the crisis is over!

Now look at those things that still scare you. Your inner child is saying, "What if this happens again?" and hears no response from you. You either believe you lack skills to keep yourself safe, or you simply haven't yet realized you need to respond to your inner child. One way or another, you are restricted in your ability to respond to harmfulness. Scare is relieved by information. There are two places to look for information, inside yourself and outside yourself. You may need to learn of options by speaking to others about your dilemma. Speak with people beyond your immediate family. Your family members may either be restricted in the same ways that you are, or they may have a vested interest in your being restricted so they can use power over you. Ask for options should this situation arise for you again. When you sigh, you know your inner child feels safe with the new options.

To solve the situation by looking inward, follow the scare back to an early life scene. Who do you blame? At the time of the event, you knew no option to protect yourself. It is your own Higher Self that has the information your feeling nature needs to feel safe. Do one or more of the processes in this book to heal yourself. Exercise new options in these scenes, and assure your inner child by telling it about other options you now have.

I grew up allowing myself only to "be nice" to others as a way of trying to prevent harmfulness to myself. Obviously, I became a doormat and an easy scapegoat. People would justify hurting me and I felt helpless to respond. I cooperated with their abuse. The message that most comforted my inner child was telling her that she does not have to be nice to people who are out to harm her. **There is an empowered response to every situation which calls for an end to harmfulness with-**

155

out doing more harm. Our challenge is to discover that response.

Use this exercise for undoing other uncomfortable feelings such as jealousy, envy, helplessness, and frustration.

C. RECEIVING YOUR GOOD

1. Seeing yourself as Beloved
Sit in front of a mirror allowing enough time to make a connection between your Higher Self and inner child. Imagine being the most loving person you could be and look at your child in the mirror with these eyes. Then switch to being the child and see that most loving person looking at you. Continue to switch back and forth allowing your feelings to flow. Typically, tears of healing flow when you see your goodness in this connection.

Be aware of the strong desire to criticize yourself. You will recognize this immediately as a demand to straighten your hair, check for bags under your eyes, and assess the pimple and wrinkle situation. All of these self-criticisms relate to trying to get love from others. **Refusal to look lovingly upon yourself is a choice to stay deprived and blame others.** Refusal to do this exercise and refusal to receive love are the same choice to blame.

2. "I Can't"
The words "I can't" are the instructions to our defense system to stay defended. In essence they say, "I *can't* open to love because I *can't* see any love there for me." When we say these words, we do not even see solutions to problems if they are right before us. We do not see options available. Or, we do not see them as possible for us even if we see them as possible for others. Know that behind these words, we are secretly or not so secretly blaming others.

Begin to reverse this pattern by listening to your speech patterns. "I can't" may be cloaked as, "I'd like to be able to."

This also says, "I am not able to." When you hear yourself say these words, change them to: "I haven't yet," "I won't," "I don't," or, "I remember doing it once. That means I can."

Behind "I can't" is a picture you hold in mind that you use to remind yourself that you aren't safe to do what your heart desires. Handle it as an early scene, release blame, and give yourself the assistance you have available through the Holy Spirit.

Another form of this is, "I can't believe that happened," or, "I can't believe this is happening." Change this to, "I can believe this and therefore I will _____ (do whatever action you see as appropriate to what is happening)." Notice that wherever you restrict your response you hold in mind a picture in which you gave up power. Go back to the scene to release blame and reclaim your power.

3. Saying "Yes" and "No"
We are saying "Yes" and "No" at all times. When we select a vanilla ice cream cone, we are saying "No" to chocolate and strawberry. **When we choose to blame, we are saying "No" to peace, love, and happiness.**

Aligning ourselves with God is a process in which we master our ability to say "No" to blame and "Yes" to our Godlike qualities. We learn to stop going along with, putting up with, giving consent to, tolerating, overlooking, participating in, and supporting things that are harmful to ourselves and others.

Our goal is to reach a point where we say "No" harmlessly with full conviction to willingly accept only that which nurtures life. The rewards are all that we long to have: security, safety, confidence, a healthy body, a light heart, and peace of mind.

All the time that we are defended we are saying "No" to going God's way. We are saying "No" to our goodness. Go through the following process to activate the right use of refusal. Refuse to defend!

157

a. Stomp around your home like a two year old stubbornly saying, "No!" "No, I won't!" and, "You can't make me!" Add to this whatever defensive behavior you seek to stop doing. For example, "No, I won't be quiet while you abuse me; try to win your love by sacrificing; spend money to try to make myself happy; or, drink, smoke, and abuse food when it is truly love I want."

b. Then walk around your home saying "No!" like a teenager does. This usually involves gestures of, "Leave me alone," and, "Get lost." Use the latest slang expressions as you refuse to do your defensive behaviors.

c. Then walk around your home saying "No" as we need to when we are around age 28-32. This is when we are preparing to express our true selves out to society instead of adapting ourselves to the "shoulds" of life as we learned them. While we follow "shoulds" to try to please others, we build resentment and blame them. We correct this by exercising our inner "No." This frees us to say "Yes" to the Holy Spirit voice.

Appropriate statements here include: "That is not right for me," "This is right for me now," "That is no longer right for me," "That is not me," "This is who I am," "That is not something I am willing to do," and, "I am willing to ____."

d. Then walk around your home saying, "I refuse to stay angry with you," "I refuse to act helpless," "I refuse to hurt myself," "I refuse to hate myself," "I refuse to hate you," "I refuse to be distracted from what I really want," "I refuse to hold myself back," "I refuse to blame you," "I refuse to stay stuck in fear," "I refuse to fix you," "I refuse to push away my good," "I refuse to stay separated from God," and, "I refuse to deny my gifts from God."

We feel safe in life as we hear our Higher Self sort out that which is and isn't right and safe for us. Sorting is also known as spiritual discernment. **Seeing the difference between light**

**and darkness and empowering our choice for light is neces-
sary to live a gentle life.** Statements of refusal in this exercise
are meant to be said with force for the purpose of building
strength into your new choices. Once clear in your thinking,
speak your messages to others without harmful intent.

4. Crooked "No's"

As children, we develop the habit of sitting on a fence as
part of pleasing others. We are afraid to say "Yes," or "No," or
state a straight stance because we want to remain free to jump
to the other side if necessary to prevent harm to ourselves.
Common language indications are: "I don't know," "I guess," "I
think," "Maybe," "Later," "We'll see," "Perhaps," "Sometime,"
"When I have time," and, "Tomorrow."

We hold pictures in our mind of being harmed if we say or
do what we truly want. The people in these pictures are more
people we blame. When we are present for our inner child, we
no longer need to sit on a fence. We are then safe to have
someone unhappy with us because we no longer believe we will
be abandoned and die if we don't please them. Decide FOR
yourself and take a stance. Nothing aligned with your Higher
Self can harm others.

5. Safe Boundaries

We all have ways in which we go out of bounds into self-
destructiveness or harmfulness. Make a list of things you do
that are not in your best interest. Then sit in front of a mirror.
Read one item and then respond with your no-nonsense Higher
Self voice that keeps you on track. Do this until you feel a
sigh. Then go to the next item on your list and repeat the process.

For example, I now realize I have a habit of saying, "My
back hurts." I see this as a defensive posture that keeps me
from being healthy, happy, and free. So, I say to the mirror, "I
say my back hurts when the truth is that I hurt emotionally."
My Higher Self responds, "Nancy, stop that!." "Nancy, speak

159

truthfully about yourself." "Nancy, let yourself be healthy, happy, and free."

6. Seal of Approval

We all wait for a seal of approval. We think we wait for this from our parents. We think we wait for this from society. We think we wait for this from God. In truth, we wait for our own approval to be and express the goodness we truly are. We release blame to receive this longed-for seal of approval.

Picture your mother and father in front of you, perhaps one at a time. See God, or any holy figure (Mary, Jesus Christ, Guardian Angel, etc.) behind them. When you are ready to look beyond your parents and express your true self directly to the holy figure, you are ready to receive the blessings of peace, love, and happiness.

When you are ready to look out to society and express your goodness rather than blame society for impacting you in harmful ways, you are ready to receive the blessings of peace, love, and happiness.

**WHEN YOU FORGIVE,
YOU SEE THAT HEAVEN SMILES ON YOU.**

MAY YOU KNOW PEACE, LOVE, AND HAPPINESS.

Nancy

18

HOPE FOR A GENTLE WORLD

*Blessed are those who hunger
and thirst for righteousness,
for they will be filled.*
Matthew 5:6

Remembering that forgiving is the only real solution to violence,
this chapter is for you to write.

Please share your results with me.

Noelani Publishing Company, Inc.
P.O. Box 24029
Cleveland, Ohio
44124-0029

**GENTLENESS IS ENTIRELY WITHIN YOUR POWER.
HOPE LIES WITHIN YOU.**

SHARING THE COURSE by Nancy H. Glende
may be obtained through:
Noelani Publishing Company, Inc.
P.O. Box 24029
Cleveland, OH, 44124-0029

Make check payable in US funds to Noelani Publishing Co.

QTY _____ at $25 each ...._____
Ohio residents add 7% tax ($1.75 per book) ...._____
Shipping first book, $3 ...._____
Shipping each additional book, $1 ...._____
                                        Total enclosed _____

        Send to:
        Name _____
        Street _____
        City _____State _____ Zip_____

Thank you for your order.

        ❊   ❊   ❊   ❊   ❊

A MUSICAL COMPANION TO SHARING THE COURSE
by Michael Root
A set of two, 40-minute audio cassette tapes with lyrics
may be obtained through:
Music of Miracles
P.O. Box 1071
Shaker Heights, OH, 44120-1071

Make check payable in US funds to Music of Miracles

QTY Tape sets _____ at $20 each ...._____
Ohio residents add 7% tax ($1.40 per set) ...._____
Shipping first set, $2 ...._____
Shipping each additional set, $1 ...._____
                                        Total enclosed _____

        Send to:
        Name _____
        Street _____
        City _____State _____ Zip_____

Thank you for your order.

FORGIVING IS THE ONLY REAL SOLUTION
TO VIOLENCE by Nancy H. Glende
may be obtained through:
Noelani Publishing Company, Inc.
P.O. Box 24029
Cleveland, OH, 44124-0029

Make check payable in US funds to Noelani Publishing Co.

QTY _____ at $14 each ...._____
Ohio residents add 7% tax ($0.98 per book) ...._____
Shipping first book, $2 ...._____
Shipping each additional book, $0.50 ...._____

Total enclosed _____

Send to:
Name _____
Street _____
City _____.State _____ Zip _____

Thank you for your order.

❋ ❋ ❋ ❋ ❋

NO MORE BLAME: A MUSICAL PROCESS OF FORGIVING AS A
WAY OUT OF VIOLENCE by Michael Root
An audio cassette tape of excerpts from MUSICAL COMPANION with
male and female solo voices. May be obtained through:
Music of Miracles
P.O. Box 1071
Shaker Heights, OH, 44120-1071

Make check payable in US funds to Music of Miracles

QTY _____ at $10 each ...._____
Ohio residents add 7% tax ($0.70 per tape) ...._____
Shipping first tape, $1.25 ...._____
Shipping each additional tape, $0.50 ...._____

Total enclosed _____

Send to:
Name _____
Street _____
City _____.State _____ Zip _____

Thank you for your order.